THE
BIBLE
OLYMPIAD

Gold Medal Trivia
for Championship Living

PAUL KENT

BARBOUR
PUBLISHING

THE
BIBLE
OLYMPIAD

© 2003 by Barbour Publishing, Inc.

ISBN 1-59310-189-9

Published by Barbour Publishing, Inc., P.O. Box 719, Uhrichsville, Ohio 44683, www.barbourbooks.com

Our mission is to publish and distribute inspirational products offering exceptional value and biblical encouragement to the masses.

ecpa Member of the
Evangelical Christian
Publishers Association

Printed in the United States of America.
5 4 3 2 1

To Mom and Dad,

who have always run well.

CONTENTS

Introduction 9
Training (Preparation) 11
Long Jump (Grasping Faith) 23
Figure Skating (God's Grace) 35
Weight Lifting (Relief in Christ) 47
Swimming (The New Life) 59
Equestrian (Trusting God) 71
Biathlon (Bible Study and Prayer) 83
Boxing (Self-Discipline) 95
Tug of War (Battling the Sin Nature) 107
Fencing (Armed with the Word) 119
Archery (Handling Temptation) 131
Skiing (Backsliding) 143
Wrestling (Spiritual Struggles) 155
Hurdles (Overcoming) 167
Balance Beam (Priorities) 179
High Jump (Striving for Excellence) 191
Marathon (Endurance) 203
The Closing Ceremony (Rewards) 215
Answers 227

CONTENTS

INTRODUCTION

Welcome, competitors—you have qualified for the Bible Olympiad!

We're all familiar with the Olympics, the quadrennial sporting event that brings the world's top athletes together for head-to-head competition. Here in the Bible Olympiad, the competition isn't against others—rather, it's designed to push you personally to ever-greater heights of Christian living.

In eighteen vital aspects of life, you'll be challenged to show your knowledge of key Bible passages. Each competition, paralleling an Olympic event, begins with a nine-point segment of Finish the Verse. That's followed by a fifteen-point quiz including Multiple Choice and Questions & Answers. The quizzes will test your memory of specific commands, warnings, and examples of Bible characters who exhibited key characteristics—both good and bad.

To earn the gold medal in each contest, you'll need at least eighteen correct answers—a 75% score. Twelve to seventeen correct answers are worth a silver medal, and six to eleven correct earns you a bronze. Less than six, and you're listed as "DNQ"—for "did not qualify." Of course, the Christian's ultimate goal is perfection, so don't ever be satisfied with any score you receive. Strive to know more—and be better—every day!

Throughout this book, you'll find "Competition Keywords" to give you an edge in each quiz. . .interesting parallels between the Christian life and the various Olympic sports. . .intriguing, and sometimes humorous, Olympic trivia. . .and profiles of "Good Sports," Olympians who showed their own Christian faith in practice or who demonstrated biblical virtues such as honesty, perseverance, and honoring others.

Are you ready to get started? Then let the games begin!

TRAINING

(Preparation)

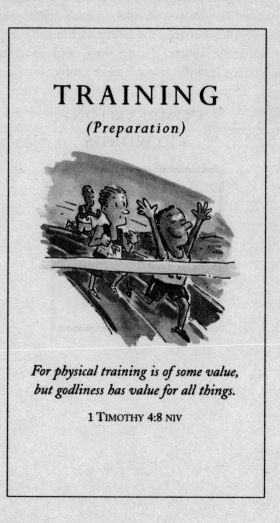

*For physical training is of some value,
but godliness has value for all things.*

1 TIMOTHY 4:8 NIV

COMPETITION
KEYWORDS

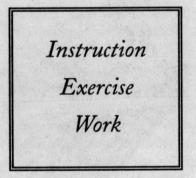

Instruction

Exercise

Work

THE OLYMPIC GAMES

For many Olympic athletes, training begins in the preschool years. It's not unusual for a figure skater to have navigated the ice shortly after learning to walk, or a swimmer to have first entered the pool as a baby.

Over the years, training programs have advanced dramatically in duration and sophistication. Participants in the first modern Olympic games, those held in the late nineteenth and early twentieth centuries, often had full-time jobs in other fields. They trained, either alone or with a private coach, as they had opportunity.

As the Olympics grew in popularity and international prestige, training programs developed as well. Whether handled as a private enterprise as in the United States or as a nationalized effort as in the former Communist nations, Olympic training became essentially a full-time job in itself. In many cases, athletes devote their entire young lives to the cause of becoming champions.

THE BIBLE OLYMPIAD

Olympic athletes often train for years, honing their skills for a particular event to have the best chance of winning a gold medal.

Here in the Bible Olympiad, training is equally vital—because the game of life will pose many difficult challenges. If you want to succeed, you'll need to know and use the Scriptures to your best advantage—as the Bible indicates in numerous passages. The training sessions that follow will test your knowledge of these very important verses.

First, in the skills training, you'll go through a workout of Finish the Verse worth a possible 9 points. After that, in the endurance training, you'll tackle Q & A and Multiple Choice worth another 15 points. You need at least 18 total points (a 75% score) to be considered a top-flight Bible Olympian for the contests to follow. Now get to work!

SKILLS TRAINING

1. Train up a child in the _____ he should go: and when he is old, he will not depart from it.

2. Ye fathers, provoke not your children to wrath: but bring them up in the nurture and admonition of the _____.

3. Whom the Lord _____ he chasteneth, and scourgeth every son whom he receiveth.

4. The grace of God that bringeth salvation hath appeared to all men, teaching us that, denying _____ and worldly lusts, we should live soberly, righteously, and godly, in this present world.

5. All Scripture is given. . .that the man of God may be perfect, thoroughly furnished unto all good _____.

6. Give instruction to a wise man, and he will be yet _____.

7. Teaching and admonishing one another in psalms and hymns and _____ songs. . .

8. Refuse profane and old wives' fables, and exercise thyself rather unto _____.

9. Work out your own salvation with fear and _____.

Answers on page 229.

Score for Skills Training: _____
  (1 point per correct answer)

ENDURANCE TRAINING

1. What, according to 1 Corinthians, is the goal of the Christian athlete's training?
    a) a home in heaven
    b) the satisfaction of Christ
    c) an incorruptible crown
    d) the Father's pleasure

2. What school-like term follows Jesus' encouragement to "take my yoke upon you"?

3. What three-letter word, describing the Ten Commandments, does Paul call a "schoolmaster" in his letter to the Galatians?

4. What did the apostle Paul tell the Romans were "for our learning, that we. . .might have hope"?
    a) "the invisible things of the creation"
    b) "whatsoever things were written aforetime"
    c) "Abraham, Isaac, and Jacob"
    d) "tribulation and anguish"

5. Who received God's promise, "I will. . .teach thee what thou shalt say," along with his calling to confront the Egyptian pharaoh?
   a) Abraham
   b) Jacob
   c) Joseph
   d) Moses

6. What prophet, who saw a great vision of God "in the year that king Uzziah died," carried the Lord's message to Israel: "Learn to do well"?

7. What four-letter word, meaning "to stand in awe," does the book of Deuteronomy five times command God's children to learn?

8. What prophet, who anointed Israel's kings Saul and David, told the Israelites "I will teach you the good and the right way: Only fear the LORD, and serve him in truth with all your heart"?

9. What follows "In all thy ways acknowledge him" in a beloved passage of Proverbs?
   a) "and he shall direct thy paths"
   b) "and he shall sustain thee"
   c) "and he shall hear thy prayers"
   d) "and he shall vindicate thee"

10. When James urges Christians not to be "hearers only" of the Word, what does he command?

11. What action on the part of Christians, according to James, will cause God to "draw nigh unto you"?
    a) "devote yourself to prayer"
    b) "give to the ministry"
    c) "spend time in the word"
    d) "draw nigh to God"

12. At what two times did the apostle Paul tell Timothy to "be instant," or prepared, to "preach the word"?

> **OLYMPIC TRIVIA**
> *The modern Olympics began in 1896 in Athens, Greece— homeland of the ancient games that originated some twenty-six hundred years earlier.*

13. What did the apostle Paul say he had learned, "in whatsoever state I am"?
    a) "to be content"
    b) "always to pray"
    c) "God is good"
    d) "faith is sufficient"

19

14. What, according to Peter, should Christians "be ready always to give" regarding "a reason of the hope that is in you"?

15. What three-word phrase completes the Lord's command in the apostle Peter's first letter: "Be ye holy; for. . ."?

Answers on pages 229–230.

Score for Endurance Training: _____
   (1 point per correct answer)

Combined score for TRAINING: _____

Points Required for Medals

Gold 18+   Silver 12–17   Bronze 6–11

RANKING: _____

GOOD SPORTS

Good Sport: Paul Anderson, U.S.A.
Site: Melbourne, Australia
Date: November 26, 1956
Event: Super Heavyweight Weight Lifting

Weighing in at 303 pounds, Paul Anderson definitely fit the title "super heavyweight." Competing with a case of strep throat, Anderson, of Toccoa, Georgia, found himself in a tough battle with an Argentinean opponent named Humberto Selvetti.

The twenty-three-year-old American came down to a single lift to determine the outcome of the competition—and dramatically succeeded in raising the 413-pound weight over his head. Though he and Selvetti ended up tied in the total amount of weight they lifted, Anderson was named the gold medalist. According to the Olympic rules, in cases of ties the lighter competitor is named the winner—and Selvetti tipped the scales at *316* pounds.

Anderson was a committed Christian who later placed his huge body into the service of others. He ran a home for troubled kids until his death in 1994.

LONG JUMP

(Grasping Faith)

*Now faith is the substance of
things hoped for,
the evidence of things not seen.*

HEBREWS 11:1

COMPETITION
KEYWORDS

Hearing

Believe

Live

THE OLYMPIC GAMES

The long jump has been part of the Olympic track and field competition since the first modern games in Athens, Greece, in 1896.

Athletes sprint down a runway at least 131 feet in length and jump from an 8-inch takeoff board, landing in a pit of sand. The jump is measured from the takeoff board to the nearest impression in the sand, whether made by the competitors' feet, hands, or backside. "Foul" jumps begin beyond the edge of the takeoff board and are not counted. In each round, competitors have three opportunities to jump, and the best effort of the three is used for placement purposes.

U.S. athletes have dominated the long jump competition. Top performers have included William DeHart Hubbard, who became the first black athlete to win an individual gold medal (at the 1924 Paris Olympics), and Bob Beamon, who broke the existing world record by nearly *two feet* when he jumped 29 feet, 2½ inches in the 1968 Mexico City games.

THE BIBLE OLYMPIAD

The long jump is, at base level, a test of an athlete's ability to leap long distances.

Here in the Bible Olympiad, you'll take a leap, too—the leap of faith. Salvation and the Christian life are not always "logical" to man's way of thinking, but God has said "my thoughts are not your thoughts, neither are your ways my ways" (Isaiah 55:8). Scripture is filled with verses that hint at the mysteries of faith. This competition will test your knowledge of these very important passages.

Your qualifying jumps will be worth 9 points, as you Finish the Verse. In the final round, you'll leap for 15 points with Q & A and Multiple Choice questions. As with each competition, you'll need at least 18 total points (a 75% score) to earn the gold medal. Take off!

QUALIFYING ROUND

1. Faith cometh by hearing, and hearing by the
   _____ _____ _____.

2. Without faith it is impossible to _____ him:
   for he that cometh to God must believe that he
   is, and that he is a rewarder of them that dili-
   gently seek him.

3. I say unto you, If ye have faith as a grain of
   _____ seed, ye shall say unto this moun-
   tain, Remove hence to yonder place; and it
   shall remove; and nothing shall be impossible
   unto you.

4. As it is written, The _____ shall live by faith.

5. Therefore being justified by faith, we have
   _____ with God through our Lord Jesus
   Christ.

6. We walk by faith, not by _____.

7. Knowing that a man is not justified by the
   works of the _____, but by the faith of Jesus
   Christ.

8. For as the body without the spirit is _____,
   so faith without works is _____ also. (Same
   word, both times.)

9. _____ yourselves, whether ye be in the faith;
   prove your own selves.

Answers on page 230.

Score for Qualifying Round: _____
   (1 point per correct answer)

Lesson 18

FINAL ROUND

1. Who does James say "believed God, and it was imputed [or credited] unto him for righteousness"?
   a) Abraham
   b) Solomon
   c) Noah
   d) Joshua

2. Who, according to the book of Hebrews, "by faith. . .offered unto God a more excellent sacrifice than Cain"?

3. What did John, in his first letter, want "you that believe on the name of the Son of God" to "know that ye have"?
   a) peace and joy
   b) eternal life
   c) comfort from the Spirit
   d) wisdom and truth

4. What, according to John's Gospel, will "whosoever believeth in him"—the only begotten Son—not do?

5. What king was first infuriated, then amazed, by the faith of Shadrach, Meshach, and Abednego, who told him, "Our God whom we serve is able to deliver us from the burning fiery furnace"?

6. Which of the following is *not* mentioned in Hebrews as a way in which faithful people of the Old Testament died?
    a) "they were stoned"
    b) "they were sawn asunder"
    c) they "were slain with the sword"
    d) "they were hanged"

7. What miracle son was Abraham willing to sacrifice, "accounting that God was able to raise him up, even from the dead"?

8. What man, according to the book of Hebrews, "by faith. . .was translated that should not see death"?
    a) Enoch
    b) David
    c) Elisha
    d) Amos

9. What sea, according to the book of Hebrews, was crossed by the Israelites, by faith, "as by dry land"?

10. What frightening phenomenon caused Jesus' disciples to fear for their lives—and brought His rebuke, "Why are ye fearful, O ye of little faith"?

11. What problem did Jesus heal two men of, saying, "According to your faith be it unto you"?
    a) leprosy
    b) blindness
    c) demon possession
    d) lameness

> **OLYMPIC TRIVIA**
> *U.S. pole-vaulter Alfred "A. C." Gilbert won a gold medal in the 1908 London Olympics, then went on to invent the popular children's toy called the Erector Set.*

12. What command, according to Mark, did Jesus make along with His invitation to "believe the gospel"?
    a) "Search the Scriptures"
    b) "Love thy brethren"
    c) "Seek truth"
    d) "Repent ye"

13. What prostitute was commended for her faith, for protecting the Israelite spies in Jericho?

14. What, according to James, must accompany faith to prove that the faith lives?

Lesson 19

15. What did Jesus say is possible "to him that believeth"?

Answers on pages 230–231.

Score for Final Round: _____
   (1 point per correct answer)

Combined score for LONG JUMP: _____

Points Required for Medals

Gold 18+   Silver 12–17   Bronze 6–11

RANKING: _____

GOOD SPORTS

Good Sport: Jim Redmond, Great Britain
Site: Barcelona, Spain
Date: August 5, 1992
Event: Men's 400 Meters

Jim Redmond didn't run in the 400-meter race in Barcelona, but his son, Derek, did. Jim was in the stands when Derek, about a third of the way into his semi-final race, tore his right hamstring in a painful injury that forced him to the ground.

As a father, Jim Redmond's first thought was to help his son—so he rushed from his seat, past the barriers and security guards, and onto the track to help Derek, who had forced himself to continue the race by hopping on his good leg. When Derek insisted on continuing his long, slow advance to the finish line, Jim Redmond said, "Okay. We started your career together, so we're going to finish this race together."

It remains one of the most poignant images in Olympic history—a compassionate father helping his injured son complete an important race. They received a standing ovation from the 65,000 fans in the Barcelona stadium.

FIGURE
SKATING

(God's Grace)

But unto every one of us is given grace.

Ephesians 4:7

COMPETITION
KEYWORDS

Gift

Mercy

Need

THE OLYMPIC GAMES

Figure skating made its first appearance in the 1908 *summer* games in London, then became an official part of the initial winter games in Chamonix, France, in 1924.

Men's singles, women's singles, pairs, and ice dancing make up the official Olympic figure skating schedule. The singles and pairs events each include two sections: a short program and a free skate. In the former, competitors must perform several required elements such as jumps and spins; in the latter, they skate their own program, showing off their talents in whatever way they choose. Judges score each performance, deducting points for errors or lack of balance in skills exhibited.

Ice dancers resemble ballroom dancers and compete in three separate events: compulsory, original, and free dances. Lifts and jumps are limited, as the focus in ice dancing falls mainly on complex footwork to match the music of the performance.

THE BIBLE OLYMPIAD

W ith its flowing movements and carefully executed jumps and spins, Olympic figure skating is a sport of tremendous grace.

Here in the Bible Olympiad, *grace* has a different meaning—it's the kindness and blessing that God shows to people who don't deserve *any* kindness or blessing. The Bible contains many verses that show God's love for undeserving humanity. . .and this competition will test your knowledge of these very encouraging passages.

First, in the short program, you'll attempt to score a perfect 9 points as you skate through Finish the Verse. In the free skate to follow, 15 points can be earned with a perfect performance in Q & A and Multiple Choice. Once again, you'll need at least 18 total points (a 75% score) to skate off with the gold medal. To the ice!

SHORT PROGRAM

1. For by grace are ye saved through _____; and that not of yourselves: it is the gift of God.

2. Let us therefore come boldly unto the _____ of grace, that we may obtain mercy, and find grace to help in time of need.

3. God resisteth the proud, but giveth grace unto the _____.

4. Grow in grace, and in the _____ of our Lord and Saviour Jesus Christ.

5. Our Lord Jesus Christ: by whom also we have access by faith into this grace wherein we _____.

6. In whom we have _____ through his blood, the forgiveness of sins, according to the riches of his grace.

7. Where _____ abounded, grace did much more abound.

8. By the grace of God _____ _____ what _____ _____: and his grace which was bestowed upon me was not in vain. (Same phrase, both times.)

9. Being _____ freely by his grace through the redemption that is in Christ Jesus.

Answers on pages 231–232.

Score for Short Program: _____
   (1 point per correct answer)

FREE SKATE

1. What word accompanies "grace" in the greeting of each of the apostle Paul's letters to churches?
   a) hope
   b) peace
   c) joy
   d) power

2. What word did Jesus use to describe his grace as it applied to the apostle Paul?

3. What physical problem, given a four-word name by the apostle Paul, led to the Lord's statement above?

4. What type of people, according to the book of James, does God give grace to?
   a) the wise
   b) the merciful
   c) the peacemakers
   d) the humble

5. What Old Testament character "found grace in the eyes of the LORD"?
    a) Adam
    b) Noah
    c) Hezekiah
    d) Solomon

6. What wayward prophet actually complained that God is "a gracious God, and merciful, slow to anger, and of great kindness"?

7. What, in addition to grace, did the apostle John say Jesus, the Word, was "full of"?
    a) truth
    b) power
    c) love
    d) hope

8. What man, whose name means "Son of Consolation (or Encouragement)," investigated the "grace of God" at Antioch, where several Greeks had accepted Christ?

9. What "overflowing" word did the apostle Paul use in Romans in connection with the grace God provides?

10. What does the apostle Paul, in the book of Romans, say Christians are *not* under, now that they are under grace?
    a) condemnation
    b) the flesh
    c) the law
    d) the curse

11. What Jewish/Gentile controversy led to Peter's declaration, "We believe that through the grace of the Lord Jesus Christ we shall be saved, even as they"?

12. What word describes the man-centered effort of earning salvation—and contradicts the idea of God's grace?

> OLYMPIC TRIVIA
> *Equipment required for the winter Olympic sport of curling includes a long sheet of ice, round granite disks with handles, and push brooms.*

13. Which of the five senses does Peter use to describe Christians' experience "that the Lord is gracious"?

14. What word, indicating good treatment of guests, does Peter mention as an example of being "good stewards of the manifold grace of God?"

15. What was the apostle Peter's command regard-
    ing grace?
    a) remember
    b) share
    c) grow in
    d) pursue

Answers on page 232.

Score for Free Skate: _____
   (1 point per correct answer)

Combined score for FIGURE SKATING
   events: _____

———————

Points Required for Medals

Gold 18+   Silver 12–17   Bronze 6–11

RANKING: _____

GOOD SPORTS

Good Sport: Inge Sorensen, Denmark
Site: Berlin, Germany
Date: August 11, 1936
Event: Women's 200-Meter Breaststroke

It's not unusual to see young athletes competing for Olympic glory—those in their teens and lower twenties often have a physical edge over the "old-timers" who've reached the ripe old age of twenty-five.

The youth movement was in full swing in the 1936 women's 200-meter breaststroke competition. Martha Geneger of the host nation, Germany, earned the silver medal at the age of fourteen. But taking the bronze was Denmark's Inge Sorensen, just twenty-four days past her twelfth birthday. She is the youngest individual medalist in Olympic history.

The youngest *gold* medalist is an American, Marjorie Gestring, who took first place in springboard diving at those same 1936 Berlin Olympics. She was thirteen years old.

WEIGHT LIFTING

(Relief in Christ)

My yoke is easy,
and my burden is light.

MATTHEW 11:30

COMPETITION
KEYWORDS

Burdens

Cast

Salvation

THE OLYMPIC GAMES

Olympic weightlifters compete in several weight categories, from men's bantamweight (approximately 123 pounds) to super heavyweight (unlimited), and from women's flyweight (approximately 106 pounds) to super heavyweight (unlimited).

Two types of lifts make up the modern weight-lifting competition: the *snatch* and the *clean and jerk*. In the snatch, lifters raise a weighted bar from the floor to above their heads in a single motion; for the lift to count, the athlete must hold the weight over his or her head for two seconds. In the clean and jerk, the weighted bar is first lifted to the chest, and then, in a second motion, raised overhead with fully extended arms. Competitors are given three attempts to success-fully complete their lifts.

Certain men's heavyweight events were held in the very first modern Olympic games, in Athens, Greece, in 1896, but most other male weight classes began com-peting in the 1920 Antwerp games. Women's weight-lifting was added to the Olympic schedule in the 2000 Sydney games.

THE BIBLE OLYMPIAD

Olympic athletes are able to lift metal bars holding amazing amounts of weight.

Here in the Bible Olympiad, Jesus Christ lifts amazing weights—His salvation removes the burden of sin, and His continuing assistance makes the trials of life bearable. Those themes occur throughout the Scriptures. This competition will test your knowledge of these important, and encouraging, passages.

You'll begin with the snatch, trying to raise 9 answers in Finish the Verse. In the clean and jerk to follow, you'll test your biblical muscle with 15 Q & A and Multiple Choice questions. As with each competition in the Bible Olympiad, you need to earn at least 18 total points (a 75% score) to carry off the gold. Happy lifting!

SNATCH

1. Cast thy burden upon the LORD, and he shall
   _____ thee.

2. Come unto me, all ye that labour and are heavy
   laden, and I will give you _____.

3. [Jesus] bare our sins in his own body on the
   _____, that we, being dead to sins, should
   live unto righteousness.

4. Surely, he hath borne our griefs, and carried
   our _____: yet we did esteem him stricken,
   smitten of God, and afflicted.

5. He hath poured out his soul unto death: and he
   was numbered with the _____; and he bare
   the sin of many, and made intercession for the
   _____. (Same word, both times.)

6. Bear ye one another's burdens, and so _____
   the law of Christ.

7. Behold, what manner of love the Father hath
   bestowed upon us, that we should be _____
   the sons of God.

8. There remaineth therefore a _____ to the people of God.

9. That it might be fulfilled which was spoken by Esaias the prophet, saying, Himself took our _____, and bare our sicknesses.

Answers on page 233.

Score for Snatch: ____
   (1 point per correct answer)

CLEAN AND JERK

1. What disciple found himself "weightless" enough to walk on water with Jesus—only as long as he kept his focus on the Lord?

2. What early Christian leader explained the way of salvation to an Ethiopian eunuch, who accepted Christ, was baptized, and "went on his way rejoicing"?
    a) Philip
    b) Andrew
    c) Nathanael
    d) Apollos

3. According to the book of Romans, "there is therefore now no" *what* "to them which are in Christ Jesus"?
    a) fear of death
    b) sorrow
    c) condemnation
    d) suffering

4. What two words, according to John, describe God in forgiving and cleansing, "if we confess our sins"?

5. How often is it, according to a psalm of David, that God "loadeth us with benefits" or "bears our burdens" (NIV)?

6. What, according to Peter's first letter, is the Christian to cast upon God?

7. What did Jesus tell believing Jews "shall make you free"?
   a) holiness
   b) mercy
   c) faith
   d) the truth

8. What type of relationship did Paul tell the Galatians their salvation gave them to God "through Christ"?
   a) friends
   b) heirs
   c) students
   d) subjects

9. When the psalmist David wrote "Bless the LORD, O my soul," what three-word phrase did he remind himself to "forget not"?

10. What adjective did the apostle Paul use to describe Christians' earthly afflictions, compared to the "far more exceeding and eternal weight of glory" to come?
    a) light
    b) unimportant
    c) worthless
    d) soft

11. What does the apostle Paul say that Jesus, "at the right hand of God. . . maketh. . . for us"?

> **OLYMPIC TRIVIA**
> *Sweden's
> silver medalist team
> in the 1968 bicycling
> time trial was
> comprised of
> four brothers.*

12. Who, according to the book of Hebrews, are "ministering spirits, sent forth to minister for them who shall be heirs of salvation"?

13. What word does Paul's letter to Titus use to describe the hope of "the glorious appearing of the great God and our Saviour Jesus Christ"?
    a) mighty
    b) blessed
    c) marvelous
    d) wondrous

14. What phrase completes Jesus' quotation: "If the Son therefore shall make you free, ye shall be. . ."?

15. What phrase completes the apostle Paul's quotation about suffering for Christ's sake: "For when I am weak. . ."?

Answers on pages 233–234.

Score for Clean and Jerk: _____
   (1 point per correct answer)

Combined score for WEIGHT LIFTING: _____

Points Required for Medals

Gold 18+   Silver 12–17   Bronze 6–11

RANKING: _____

GOOD SPORTS

Good Sport: Ronald Weigel, East Germany
Site: Seoul, South Korea
Date: September 23, 1988
Event: Men's 20,000-Meter Walk

In the little known 20,000-meter walk, a grueling race of more than twelve miles, Weigel earned the silver medal. He finished in one hour and twenty minutes, only three seconds behind the gold medalist, Jozef Pribilinec, a Slovak competing for the Czech Republic.

After crossing the finish line, the weary Pribilinec fell the ground and lay flat on his back. Weigel, wanting to congratulate Pribilinec on his victory, knelt over the Slovak to offer a word of praise—but Pribilinec was so exhausted that he couldn't acknowledge the East German's kindness.

Photographers caught Weigel's sportsmanship on film as he leaned over Pribilinec, placed a congratulatory kiss on his cheek, and then quietly walked away.

SWIMMING

(The New Life)

For the Lamb...
will lead them to springs of living water.

REVELATION 7:17 NIV

COMPETITION
KEYWORDS

Water

Clean

Life

THE OLYMPIC GAMES

Swimming events, at least for men, have been part of the Olympics since the first modern games in Greece in 1896.

Participants in those early games swam outdoors in the cold waters of the bay at Piraeus. Olympians now swim in pools that must be 50 meters (approximately 164 feet) in length.

Both men and women swimmers, who first took part in the 1912 Stockholm Olympics, compete in several types of races, including the freestyle, backstroke, breaststroke, and butterfly. So-called "medley" races feature a mixture of the various styles. Distances covered range from 50 meters to 1,500 meters, or slightly less than a mile.

Olympic swimming lore includes the amazing performance of American Mark Spitz, who won a record *seven* gold medals at the 1972 Munich games. Two other American gold medalists—Johnny Weissmuller in 1928 and Buster Crabbe in 1932—turned their swimming successes into Hollywood stardom, as they went on to portray Tarzan on film.

THE BIBLE OLYMPIAD

In Olympic swimming contests, success comes to those who best adapt to the foreign environment of water.

Here in the Bible Olympiad, you'll face a similar adaptation process—as you begin to move into a new world of God's love and grace. The Bible is filled with verses that describe this new life, often connecting the new life with water. This competition will test your knowledge of these important passages.

In the semifinal race, you'll swish your way through a course of Finish the Verse worth a possible 9 points. In the finals, Multiple Choice and Q & A offer the potential for another 15 points. As always, you'll need at least 18 total points (a 75% score) to win the gold medal. Splash in!

SEMIFINALS

1. Whosoever drinketh of the water that I shall give him shall never _____.

2. He that believeth on me, as the _____ hath said, out of his belly shall flow rivers of living water.

3. With joy shall ye draw water out of the wells of _____.

4. Though our outward man perish, yet the inward man is _____ day by day.

5. We know that we have passed from death unto life, because we _____ the brethren.

6. Create in me a clean heart, O God; and renew a _____ spirit within me.

7. Not by works of righteousness which we have done, but according to his mercy he saved us, by the _____ of regeneration, and renewing of the Holy Ghost.

8. Put on the new man, which after God is created in righteousness and true _____.

9. The water that I shall give him shall be in him a well of water springing up into _____ life.

Answers on page 234.

Score for Semifinals: ___

   (1 point per correct answer)

FINALS

1. What two-word phrase did the apostle Paul use to describe "if any man be in Christ"?

2. What type of heart, according to the Book of Ezekiel, does God replace when He says "a new spirit will I put within you"?
   a) of iron
   b) stony
   c) ice cold
   d) of wood

3. What two substances did Jesus say a person must be "born of" to enter the kingdom of God?

4. What man, visiting Jesus at night, heard salvation described as being "born again"?
   a) Nicodemus
   b) Zacchaeus
   c) Lazarus
   d) Joseph of Arimathea

5. What kind of life did Jesus promise to those who know "the only true God, and Jesus Christ, whom thou hast sent"?

6. Who did Jesus use as an object lesson to illustrate His comment to the disciples, "Except ye be converted. . .ye shall not enter into the kingdom of heaven"?

7. Which of the disciples said to Jesus, "Thou hast the words of eternal life"?
   a) John
   b) Peter
   c) James
   d) Andrew

8. Which of the following, from Jesus' parable of the sower, is *not* among the crop yields of the person who "heareth the word, and understandeth it; which also beareth fruit"?
   a) 250 times
   b) 100 times
   c) 60 times
   d) 30 times

9. What wealthy tax collector proved his conversion by promising to give half his possessions to the poor and to pay back four times any money he had gained through cheating?

10. Where was the persecutor Saul traveling to when he was stopped by the Lord and converted to Christianity?

11. In what city did Silas and Paul—the former persecutor Saul—lead the local jailer to life in Christ?
    a) Troas
    b) Berea
    c) Philippi
    d) Athens

OLYMPIC TRIVIA
The full name of the United States' gold medalist in the 1912 Stockholm and 1920 Antwerp 100-meter freestyle swimming competitions: Duke Paoa Kahinu Makoe Hulikohoa Kahanamoku. If you guessed he was born in Hawaii, you're right!

12. When Jesus said, "no man cometh unto the Father, but by me," what two names did He give Himself besides "the life"?

13. What does John's first letter say proves "that we have passed from death unto life"?
    a) "we tithe our income"
    b) "we love the brethren"
    c) "we entertain strangers"
    d) "we read the Scriptures"

14. How did Jesus say He came to provide life for His sheep?

15. When the apostle Paul wrote that "to live is Christ," what did he say it is to die?

Answers on pages 234–235.

Score for Finals: _____

(1 point per correct answer)

Combined score for SWIMMING: _____

Points Required for Medals

Gold 18+   Silver 12–17   Bronze 6–11

RANKING: _____

GOOD SPORTS

Good Sport: Jack Keller, U.S.A.
Site: Los Angeles, California
Date: August 3, 1932
Event: Men's 110-Meter Hurdles

The innovation of the photo-finish camera was introduced to track and field events at the 1932 Los Angeles games, and it worked to the disadvantage of American hurdler Jack Keller.

Keller and two other runners, Donald Finlay and David Burghley of Great Britain, all finished the course in 14.8 seconds, just slightly off the pace set by two other Americans, gold medalist George Saling and silver winner Percy Beard. Judges deemed Keller the first across the line after Beard and awarded him the bronze.

When the film of the race was reviewed, Olympic officials decided that Finlay had actually edged Keller and announced that the Briton should be the bronze medalist. When he heard the news, Keller found Finlay in the Olympic village and personally presented him with the third-place medal.

EQUESTRIAN

(Trusting God)

Some trust in chariots and some in horses,
but we trust in the name of
the LORD our God.

PSALM 20:7 NIV

COMPETITION
KEYWORDS

Help

Peace

Victory

THE OLYMPIC GAMES

Olympic equestrian events include several tests of endurance and skill for both horse and rider.

Jumping events, first held at the 1900 Paris Olympics, require horses and riders to hurdle several obstacles between 4 foot 7 inches and 5 feet 3 inches tall. Penalties are given for any horse that knocks down an obstacle, falls, or refuses to attempt the jump.

Dressage is a test of a horse's obedience, with competitors judged on how the animal responds to the rider's commands. This event first appeared at the 1912 Stockholm games.

The three-day event combines dressage and jumping with a four-part endurance test with races ranging in distance from about two and a half to five miles. The three-day event, first appearing at the 1912 Stockholm games, is so grueling that through the 1968 Mexico City games several horses died in the competition.

THE BIBLE OLYMPIAD

Trust is essential in Olympic equestrian events—the horse must trust its rider, and the rider his or her horse.

Here in the Bible Olympiad, trust is vital, as well. But you won't be trusting in horses or chariots, as Psalm 20:7 indicates—all trust is properly directed to God Himself. The Bible is packed with encouragement to trust God. This competition will test your knowledge of these key passages.

Your first event in this competition, dressage, is a round of Finish the Verse worth 9 points. After that, the three-day event will test you with Multiple Choice and Q & A for another 15 points. Remember—you need at least 18 total points (a 75% score) to take home the gold. Saddle up!

DRESSAGE

1. Trust in the LORD with all thine heart; and _____ not unto thine own understanding.

2. It is better to trust in the LORD than to put confidence in _____.

3. O my God, I trust in thee: let me not be _____, let not mine enemies triumph over me.

4. Trust in the LORD, and do _____.

5. O LORD of hosts, _____ is the man that trusteth in thee.

6. The fear of man bringeth a _____: but whoso putteth his trust in the LORD shall be safe.

7. What time I am _____, I will trust in thee.

8. God is our refuge and _____, a very present help in trouble.

9. Trust in him at _____ _____; ye people, pour out your heart before him: God is a refuge for us.

Answers on pages 235–236.

Score for Dressage: _____

(1 point per correct answer)

THREE-DAY EVENT

1. What Old Testament figure uttered the famous
   words, "Though he [God] slay me, yet will I
   trust in him"?
   a) Abraham
   b) Job
   c) Daniel
   d) Joseph

2. What stringed weapon did the psalmist say he
   would *not* put his trust in, realizing that God
   gives the victory?

3. To what protective cover did King David, flee-
   ing his treasonous son Absalom, compare God?
   a) helmet
   b) wall
   c) hedge
   d) shield

4. What word—also applied to the serpent in
   Genesis—does Jeremiah use to describe "the
   man that trusteth in man"?

5. Who did King Nebuchadnezzar praise for trusting God rather than fearing the fiery furnace?

6. Trusting in what, according to Jesus, makes it "hard" to enter the kingdom of God?
    a) good deeds
    b) riches
    c) human wisdom
    d) kings of earth

7. Who used the words "He trusted in God" as a mocking insult of Jesus during the Crucifixion?

8. To what beloved hill, which "abideth for ever," are those who trust in the Lord compared?

9. What king of Judah "trusted in the LORD God of Israel"—and was rewarded with an extra fifteen years of life?
    a) Hezekiah
    b) Manasseh
    c) Asa
    d) Jehoshaphat

10. What protective structures, which proved inadequate for Jericho, did God warn Israel against trusting in?

11. What word, according to Psalm 40, describes the man who "maketh the LORD his trust"?
    a) honorable
    b) wise
    c) blessed
    d) powerful

12. What jealous king had David escaped from when he sang, "The LORD is my rock. . .in him will I trust"?

13. What adopted homeland did Moses leave, choosing to follow God rather than enjoy "the pleasures of sin for a season"?
    a) Assyria
    b) Babylon
    c) Egypt
    d) Philistia

OLYMPIC TRIVIA
Lynette Woodard, a member of the gold medalist U.S. women's basketball team at the 1984 Los Angeles Olympics, became the first female member of the Harlem Globetrotters.

14. What strong word do the Proverbs use to describe a man who "trusts in himself" (NIV)?

15. What kind of peace, according to Isaiah, will God give the man who "trusteth in thee"?

Answers on page 236.

Score for Three-Day Event: _____
   (1 point per correct answer)

Combined score for EQUESTRIAN: _____

Points Required for Medals

Gold 18+   Silver 12–17   Bronze 6–11

RANKING: _____

GOOD SPORTS

Good Sport: Carl Ludwig "Luz" Long, Germany
Site: Berlin, Germany
Date: August 4, 1936
Event: Men's Long Jump

Propaganda was the name of the game in 1936, as German dictator Adolf Hitler used the Berlin Olympics to push his views of "Aryan supremacy." Hitler and his Nazi officials wanted the world to see the superiority of their blond haired, blue-eyed athletes over those of other nations and races, especially over Jews and blacks.

But at least one German athlete didn't buy into Hitler's philosophy: Long jumper Luz Long. Finding the black American Jesse Owens nervous and rattled in the qualifying jumps, Long offered his friendship—and some advice—that helped Owens not only to qualify, but to win the gold medal with an Olympic record jump of 26 feet, 5$\frac{1}{2}$ inches. Long earned the silver, with a jump that was seven and a half inches shorter.

When Owens clinched first place on his final jump, Long rushed to congratulate him—within the clear view of Hitler. Owens later claimed the gold of his medals couldn't compare to the "twenty-four-carat friendship" he felt for Long.

BIATHLON

(Bible Study and Prayer)

Search the Scriptures.
Every one that is godly pray.

JOHN 5:39, PSALM 32:6

COMPETITION
KEYWORDS

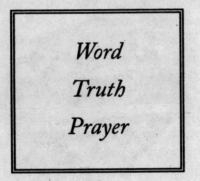

Word

Truth

Prayer

THE OLYMPIC GAMES

The name "biathlon" comes from Greek words indicating "two contests."

In the Winter Olympics, the biathlon is an event that includes both cross-country skiing and rifle shooting. The competition was first held at the 1960 games in Squaw Valley, California. Four races—the sprint, the pursuit, the individual, and the relay—make up the Olympic biathlon schedule.

Each biathlon race features a cross-country ski course, ranging in length from about 4.7 to 18.6 miles. Competitors stop at prearranged locations to fire at rifle targets; in three of the four races, they can only use five bullets to hit the five targets. Misses incur penalties: either minutes added to their overall times or the skiing of a 150-meter penalty loop.

Races are held for both men and women. Each women's race is slightly shorter than its men's counterpart.

THE BIBLE OLYMPIAD

To compete effectively, Olympic biathletes must excel at two separate disciplines.

Here in the Bible Olympiad, you'll need to master twin disciplines, as well. To succeed in the game of life, you'll have to excel in both Bible study and prayer. The Bible is full of commands and encouragement to pursue both activities. This competition will test your knowledge of these vital passages.

In the first event, cross-country skiing, you'll work your way through Finish the Verse worth a possible 9 points. Along the way, you'll fire your rifle at 15 targets in the Q & A and Multiple Choice. You need to tally at least 18 total points (a 75% score) to earn the gold medal. To the starting line!

CROSS-COUNTRY SKIING

1. Thy word is a _____ unto my feet.

2. Thy word have I hid in my heart, that I might not _____ against thee.

3. Let the word of Christ dwell in you _____.

4. Whatsoever things were written aforetime were written for our learning, that we through patience and comfort of the scriptures might have _____.

5. From a child thou hast known the holy scriptures, which are able to make thee _____ unto salvation through faith which is in Christ Jesus.

6. If any of you lack _____, let him ask of God. . .and it shall be given him.

7. The effectual fervent prayer of a _____ man availeth much.

8. If we ask anything according to his _____, he heareth us.

9. _____ them that curse you, and pray for them which despitefully use you.

Answers on page 237.

Score for Cross-Country Skiing: _____

    (1 point per correct answer)

RIFLE SHOOTING

1. What city's residents are described in the Book of Acts as "noble" for testing Paul's preaching against the Scriptures?

2. What word completes Jesus' quote, "Thy word is. . ."?
    a) wisdom
    b) power
    c) hope
    d) truth

3. What word, according to Paul's letter to Timothy, describes the studying Christian, "rightly dividing the word of truth"?

4. What, according to Hebrews, is the Word of God sharper than?
    a) a spear
    b) a flint
    c) a twoedged sword
    d) a thorn

5. In what part of their houses were the ancient Israelites to write God's commands, as a daily reminder to themselves and their children?

6. To what liquid did both Paul and Peter liken the Word?
   a) milk
   b) oil
   c) water
   d) wine

7. What Old Testament priest, for whom a Bible book is named, worked with Nehemiah to encourage the public reading and study of Scripture?

8. What Old Testament character regularly prayed three times a day—even though it got him in trouble?
   a) Moses
   b) Joshua
   c) Daniel
   d) Jonah

9. What "I" word describes the Holy Spirit's assistance in the Christian's prayers?

10. What phrase follows "Our Father, which art in heaven" in Jesus' model prayer?
    a) "thy kingdom come"
    b) "hallowed be thy name"
    c) "thy will be done"
    d) "forgive us our debts"

11. What two verbs, after "ask," complete Jesus' instruction on prayer to His disciples?

12. With what two-word phrase, found several times in the book of John, did Jesus encourage his disciples to "ask in"?

13. What kind of bread did Jesus teach his disciples to pray for, asking God to "give us this day"?

> OLYMPIC TRIVIA
> *Cricket and croquet were official events only at the 1900 Paris games. Motor boating made its only appearance at the 1908 London games.*

14. Who pestered an unjust judge in Jesus' parable that taught his disciples "always to pray, and not to faint," or "give up" (NIV)?

15. How, according to the apostle Paul, are Christians to pray?
    a) without pride
    b) without ceasing
    c) without hypocrisy
    d) without wavering

Answers on pages 237–238.

Score for Rifle Shooting: _____
   (1 point per correct answer)

Combined score for BIATHLON: _____

Points Required for Medals

Gold 18+   Silver 12–17   Bronze 6–11

RANKING: _____

GOOD SPORTS

Good Sport: Heather "Judy" Guinness, Great Britain
Site: Los Angeles, California
Date: August 3, 1932
Event: Women's Foil

Every Olympic competitor dreams of winning a gold medal. But for England's Judy Guinness, the dream of a first-place finish couldn't outweigh the importance of a fair and honest competition.

In the fencing event called the foil, competitors try to score "touches" against their opponents. Guinness notified the judges of two touches on her that they had failed to notice. Those two points became the margin of victory for Ellen Preis of Austria, who won the match 5-3. Had she not spoken out, Guinness would have been tied—and had the opportunity to pursue winning touches against Preis.

Guinness would never again have the opportunity to compete for a gold medal.

BOXING

(Self-Discipline)

Fight the good fight of faith.

1 TIMOTHY 6:12

COMPETITION
KEYWORDS

Fight

Strive

Sober

THE OLYMPIC GAMES

Boxing events were first held in the 1904 St. Louis Olympics, though the competitors participating were all from the United States. True international competition began at the 1908 London games.

Boxers "pick on someone their own size" by fighting within several weight classes—from light flyweight (about 105 pounds) through super heavyweight (unlimited weight). Battling in a twenty-foot-square ring, boxers have traditionally competed in three three-minute rounds, though in the 2000 Sydney Olympics the format was changed to four two-minute rounds.

By nature a violent sport, boxing has a number of rules to protect competitors' safety: Boxers must be between the ages of 17 and 34, protective headgear is required, and referees can stop the match at any time to protect a competitor knocked down or stunned by blows. Multiple "eight count" breaks, or a single "ten count," spell defeat for a dazed boxer; if neither boxer "knocks out" his opponent, a five-member panel of judges decides the winner.

THE BIBLE OLYMPIAD

Years of self-discipline—in diet, exercise, and training—precede any boxer's appearance in the Olympics.

Here in the Bible Olympiad, self-discipline is another key factor in your ultimate success. You'll need to be the kind of person the Bible describes as "sober," "temperate," and "self-controlled." In fact, the pages of Scripture are filled with commands to discipline oneself and examples of those who did—and didn't. The following competition will test your knowledge of these passages.

In the preliminary match, you'll spar to Finish the Verse for a possible 9 points. After that, in the championship match, you'll be tested by Q & A and Multiple Choice worth another 15 points. As always, you need at least 18 total points (a 75% score) to win the gold medal. Knock 'em out!

PRELIMINARY MATCH

1. So fight I, not as one that beateth the air: But I keep under my body, and bring it into _____.

2. They that are Christ's have _____ the flesh with the affections and lusts.

3. Whosoever he be of you that forsaketh not all that he hath, he cannot be my _____.

4. Then said Jesus unto his disciples, If any man will come after me, let him _____ himself, and take up his cross, and follow me.

5. This I say then, Walk in the _____, and ye shall not fulfil the lust of the flesh.

6. He that hath no rule over his own spirit is like a city that is broken down, and without _____.

7. Let not sin therefore _____ in your mortal body, that ye should obey it in the lusts thereof.

8. Every man that striveth for the mastery is temperate in _____ _____.

9. Denying ungodliness and worldly lusts, we should live soberly, _____, and godly, in this present world.

Answers on page 238.

Score for Preliminary Match: _____

    (1 point per correct answer)

CHAMPIONSHIP MATCH

1. What over-indulgers in food, according to the Proverbs, should be avoided?

2. What Old Testament figure chose vegetables and water over his king's meat and wine?
   a) Moses
   b) Daniel
   c) David
   d) Jeremiah

3. What discipline, along with prayer, did Jesus say was necessary for His disciples to cast out a "dumb and deaf spirit"?
   a) obedience
   b) forgiving
   c) fasting
   d) tithing

4. What Old Testament vow of separation to God forbade the taking of "wine and strong drink" or "any liquor of grapes"?

5. What otherwise faithful man once had an embarrassing episode of drunkenness in his tent?
    a) Moses
    b) Joshua
    c) Joseph
    d) Noah

6. What part of the body, according to James, "can no man tame"?

7. What quality in a man, according to the Proverbs, makes him "better than the mighty"?

8. What did David take from an unsuspecting King Saul, rather than killing him as David's men urged?
    a) a lock of his hair
    b) a corner of his robe
    c) an arrow from his quiver
    d) a strap from his sandal

9. To what kind of animal is the devil compared, when Peter urges Christians to "be sober, be vigilant"?

10. What group of church leaders, according to Paul, must have wives who are "grave. . .sober, faithful in all things"?

11. Which of the following is *not* listed with temperance (or self-control) in the nine-fold listing of the "fruit of the Spirit"?
    a) wisdom
    b) love
    c) peace
    d) goodness

> **OLYMPIC TRIVIA**
> *American Ray Ewry was called "The Human Frog" for his abilities in the now discontinued standing high jump. His jump of 5' 5" in the 1900 Paris Olympics is even more impressive considering the childhood polio he had suffered.*

12. Which of the disciples told Jesus they had "left all" to follow him—and heard Jesus promise a hundred-fold return?
    a) Peter
    b) Judas Iscariot
    c) Matthew
    d) John

13. What Roman governor, interviewing the prisoner Paul, dismissed the apostle when he began to talk of "righteousness, temperance, and judgment to come"?

14. What seven-letter word, which can also mean "to embarrass," does the apostle Paul use when telling Christians to put to death their earthly desires?

15. What extreme advice did Jesus have for a person whose "right hand offend thee"—indicating the seriousness of dealing with sin?

Answers on pages 238–239.

Score for Championship Match: _____
   (1 point per correct answer)

Combined score for BOXING: _____

Points Required for Medals

Gold 18+   Silver 12–17   Bronze 6–11

RANKING: _____

GOOD SPORTS

Good Sport: Karoly Takacs, Hungary
Site: London, England
Date: August 4, 1948
Event: Men's Rapid-Fire Pistol

Military service provided an opportunity for Karoly Takacs, a member of Hungary's world champion shooting team, to continually polish his skills. But that same military service became an obstacle to Takacs's Olympic hopes, when a grenade accidentally exploded in his shooting hand. It was completely destroyed.

Takacs took the disaster in stride, though, and began teaching himself to shoot with his other hand. Ten years later, he earned a spot on Hungary's Olympic team, and then won the gold medal in London, setting a world record at the same time.

To prove that the first-place finish was no fluke, Takacs also took gold in the next Olympic games, held in Helsinki, Finland, in 1952.

TUG OF WAR

(Battling the Sin Nature)

I do not understand what I do.
For what I want to do I do not do,
but what I hate I do.

ROMANS 7:15 NIV

COMPETITION
KEYWORDS

Sin
Flesh
Transformed

THE OLYMPIC GAMES

Though it may seem strange today, tug of war was an official sport in the early years of the Olympics.

Considered a part of the track and field program, tug of war appeared in the 1900, 1904, 1908, 1912, and 1920 games. Teams of eight men each would take position at the ends of a long rope and attempt to pull their opponents six feet forward to earn victory. If neither team could pull the other six feet within five minutes, the team that pulled the other the farthest was declared the winner.

As often happened in the early Olympics, some of the tug of war events featured multiple teams from the host nation. Such was the case with the 1904 St. Louis Olympics, when U.S. teams won the top four places, and in the 1908 London Olympics, when three British teams swept the field. One of those British teams, easily defeating the U.S. squad, was accused by the Americans of using illegally spiked boots. The British, asserting their innocence, challenged the U.S. team to a tug of war to be held in stocking feet—though historians find no evidence of this event taking place.

THE BIBLE OLYMPIAD

Old photographs show Olympic tug of war competitors straining and pulling, trying to gain the upper hand in their athletic contest.

Here in the Bible Olympiad, you'll experience the tug of war, too—that internal battle between good and evil that challenges every Christian who wants to live faithfully. Commands to reject the wrong and embrace the right fill the pages of Scripture, while stories of people who did and didn't follow those commands provide examples for us today. This competition will test your knowledge of these important passages.

In the preliminary pull, you'll vie for 9 points in Finish the Verse. The championship pull is worth a potential 15 points, with Q & A and Multiple Choice. Keep in mind that you'll need at least 18 total points (a 75% score) to win gold.

Pull away!

PRELIMINARY PULL

1. Knowing this, that our old man is _____ with him, that the body of sin might be destroyed, that henceforth we should not serve sin.

2. I beseech you as strangers and pilgrims, abstain from fleshly lusts, which _____ against the soul.

3. _____ not one to another, seeing that ye have put off the old man with his deeds.

4. I know that in me (that is, in my flesh,) dwelleth no _____ thing.

5. With the mind I myself serve the _____ of God; but with the flesh the _____ of sin. (Same word, both times.)

6. I find then a law, that, when I would do good, _____ is present with me.

7. He should no longer live the rest of his time in the flesh to the lusts of men, but to the _____ of God.

8. I am crucified with Christ: nevertheless I
    _____; yet not I, but Christ liveth in me.

9. I have set before you life and death, blessing and
    cursing; therefore _____ life, that both thou
    and thy seed may live.

Answers on pages 239–240.

Score for Preliminary Pull: _____

    (1 point per correct answer)

CHAMPIONSHIP PULL

1. What three-letter adjective describes "man" in the apostle Paul's letters to describe the former life of sin?

2. What two disciples let their anger get the best of them by suggesting that a Samaritan village that had snubbed Jesus be destroyed by fire from heaven?

3. How did Jesus respond to His disciples' comment above?
   a) He wept
   b) He rebuked them
   c) He prayed
   d) He ignored them

4. What, according to Romans 8:8, can "they that are in the flesh" not do?
   a) enter heaven
   b) enjoy favor
   c) please God
   d) obtain peace

5. What apostle angrily called the high priest Ananias a "whited wall"—then admitted he was wrong to do so?
    a) Paul
    b) Peter
    c) Andrew
    d) Matthew

6. When Paul told the Romans "be not conformed to this world," how did he tell them to be transformed?

7. What did the apostle Paul tell the Corinthians they should bring "into captivity"?

8. What word, which Jeremiah used to describe the human heart, did the apostle Paul also use to describe the lusts that corrupt?

9. What man succumbed to the temptation to misrepresent an offering he had made to the early church—with deadly results?
    a) Demetrius
    b) Ananias
    c) Cornelius
    d) Apollos

10. What "W" word does Paul use in Romans 7 to describe himself when torn between doing good and evil?

11. What did Paul notice that Peter stopped doing with Gentiles at Antioch when a group of circumcised Jews arrived?
    a) discussing Scripture
    b) eating
    c) conducting business
    d) worshiping

12. What does John, in his first letter, tell Christians to "love not"?

> **OLYMPIC TRIVIA**
> *Light heavyweight wrestlers Anders Ahlgren of Sweden and Ivar Bohling of Finland battled for nine hours in the 1912 Stockholm Olympics before officials called the match a draw.*

13. What does Paul tell the Romans to "mortify," or put to death, through God's Spirit?
    a) "the thoughts of the mind"
    b) "the desires of the heart"
    c) "the wants of the soul"
    d) "the deeds of the body"

14. What did Peter encourage believers to "make your calling and election"?

15. When the apostle Paul urged Roman Christians to "cast off the works of darkness," what did he encourage them to put on instead?

Answers on page 240.

Score for Championship Pull: _____
(1 point per correct answer)

Combined score for TUG OF WAR: _____

Points Required for Medals

Gold 18+   Silver 12–17   Bronze 6–11

RANKING: _____

GOOD SPORTS

Good Sport: Robert Van Osdel, U.S.A.
Site: Los Angeles, California
Date: July 31, 1932
Event: Men's High Jump

At the University of Southern California, Robert Van Osdel and Canadian high jumper Duncan McNaughton were good friends. Van Osdel, an experienced high jumper, had taken on McNaughton as an informal coaching project.

When the Los Angeles Olympics came around, McNaughton begged the Canadian officials for a spot on the team and ultimately worked his way into gold medal contention. Van Osdel, also in the running for first place, gave McNaughton some advice on his technique that helped the Canadian clear the bar at 6 feet, 5½ inches and win the top prize.

In an interesting footnote to their story, McNaughton's gold medal was stolen a year later. Van Osdel, by that time a dentist, made a replacement for his friend by creating a cast of his own silver medal and pouring in molten gold.

FENCING

(Armed with the Word)

Take. . .the sword of the Spirit,
which is the word of God.

EPHESIANS 6:17

COMPETITION KEYWORDS

Law

Prophecy

Scripture

THE OLYMPIC GAMES

Fencing is a type of sword fighting—though in the Olympics, the goal of the competitors is simply to register "hits," or touches, on their opponents.

Three separate competitions are held, each named for a type of sword: the *foil*, with its blunt, flexible, rectangular blade; the *épée*, with its rigid triangular blade and cone-covered point; and the *saber*, with its blunt-pointed, flexible triangular blade. Matches are played to fifteen points, with hits being scored for touches to the torso in foil competition, to any part of the body in épée, and to any part of the body above the waist (including the head and arms) in saber.

Men's foil and saber appeared in the first modern Olympics, in Athens, Greece, in 1896, while the épée was added to the second modern Olympiad, in 1900 in Paris. Women's foil was added to the Paris games of 1924, and épée to the 1996 Atlanta games. To this point, women have not competed with sabers.

THE BIBLE OLYMPIAD

In the Olympic fencing competition, agility and quickness are essential—and so is a sword.

Here in the Bible Olympiad, you'll need similar flair to handle your sword—which, according to Ephesians 6:17, is the word of God. The Bible is full of instruction on why and how to use its knowledge in the battles of life. This competition will test your knowledge of these vital passages.

In your first event, the foil, you'll Finish the Verse for a possible 9 points. Next, in the épée, you'll lunge and parry your way through Q & A and Multiple Choice questions, worth another 15 points. As always, you'll need at least 18 total points (a 75% score) to win the gold medal. *En garde!*

FOIL

1. I am not ashamed of the gospel of Christ: for it
   is the _____ of God unto salvation to every
   one that believeth.

2. The word of the Lord endureth _____
   _____.

3. All scripture is given by _____ of God, and is
   profitable for doctrine, for reproof, for correc-
   tion, for instruction in righteousness.

4. Heaven and earth shall _____ _____; but
   my words shall not _____ _____. (Same
   phrase, both times.)

5. The law of the LORD is _____, converting
   the soul.

6. These things have I written unto you that
   believe on the name of the Son of God; that ye
   may know that ye have _____ _____.

7. Sanctify them through thy _____: thy word is
   _____. (Same word, both times.)

8. Prophecy came not in old time by the _____ of man: but holy men of God spake as they were moved by the Holy Ghost.

9. O how love I thy law! it is my _____ all the day.

Answers on page 241.

Score for Foil: _____

    (1 point per correct answer)

ÉPÉE

1. What did the psalmist say God's Word was sweeter than "to my mouth"?

2. What tool "that breaketh the rock in pieces" does the book of Jeremiah liken God's Word to?

3. What do the Proverbs call the person who tries to add to God's Words?
   a) a liar
   b) a fool
   c) a cheat
   d) a devil

4. What New Testament writer warned readers against adding to or taking away from the words of his book?
   a) Matthew
   b) James
   c) Peter
   d) John

5. What Old Testament prophet's writing did Jesus read aloud in the Nazareth synagogue, telling the people "This day is this scripture fulfilled in your ears"?
   a) Ezekiel
   b) Esaias, or Isaiah
   c) Hosea
   d) Jeremy, or Jeremiah

6. What did Jesus once say that Scripture cannot be?

7. What great king of Israel did Jesus once quote from the Book of Psalms?

8. Which of the following is *not* among the portions of the Old Testament that Jesus said "were written. . .concerning me"?
   a) the law of Moses
   b) the prophets
   c) the psalms
   d) the proverbs

9. What did Jesus, quoting Deuteronomy 8:3, say that "man shall not live by" when He said that man *should* live by "every word of God"?

10. What three-letter synonym for God's Word appears some two dozen times in Psalm 119?

11. What young king of Judah renewed the covenant with God after workmen found "the book of the law" while repairing the temple?
    a) Josiah
    b) Ahaz
    c) Manasseh
    d) Amon

12. Whose biblical writings, according to Peter, contain "some things hard to be understood" which are distorted by "they that are unlearned and unstable"?
    a) Moses
    b) Isaiah
    c) Paul
    d) James

> **OLYMPIC TRIVIA**
> *Ice hockey was part of the 1920* summer *Olympics held in Antwerp, Belgium.*

13. What is one of the two short-lived plants, which "withereth" and "fadeth," that Isaiah contrasts with the everlasting Word of God?

14. What two words, indicating tiny strokes of the pen, did Jesus say would not "pass from the law, till all be fulfilled"?

15. What word, also used in triplicate to describe the Lord God Almighty, did the apostle Paul use to describe the law?

Answers on pages 241–242.

Score for Épée: _____

   (1 point per correct answer)

Combined score for FENCING: _____

Points Required for Medals

Gold 18+   Silver 12–17   Bronze 6–11

RANKING: _____

GOOD SPORTS

Good Sport: Mary Lou Retton, U.S.A.
Site: Los Angeles, California
Date: August 3, 1984
Event: Women's All-Around Gymnastics

In the first thirty-two years of the women's all-around gymnastics competition, no American had even finished in the top eight, let alone earned a medal. Then, in 1984, Mary Lou Retton appeared on the scene.

Sixteen years old, standing only four feet, eight inches tall, and weighing less than one hundred pounds, Retton had the advantage of not facing a Soviet opponent, since the U.S.S.R. was boycotting the Los Angeles games. But she still had formidable competition in a pair of Romanians, in recent years the Soviet's top challengers. By turning in scores of perfect 10s in both the vault and the floor exercise, though, Retton was able to give the U.S. its first-ever gold medal in the all-around competition.

Retton became a darling of the American media and endorsed products from cereal to batteries. In recent years, she's written a Christian book and produced a television series for children.

ARCHERY

(Handling Temptation)

*You can extinguish all
the flaming arrows of the evil one.*

EPHESIANS 6:16 NIV

COMPETITION
KEYWORDS

Lusts

Yield

Deliver

THE OLYMPIC GAMES

Olympic archery events test a competitor's skill with the bow and arrow.

Using high-tech bows, archers shoot at a target that's four feet in diameter and marked with five colored rings. Competitors earn more points for arrows that land closer to the center of the target; the gold bull's-eye in the center is less than five inches wide. Archers shoot from distances of 30 to 90 meters (about 98 to 295 feet). Events are held for both men and women, singly and in teams.

Archery is a relative newcomer to the Olympics, gaining a firm spot in the 1972 Munich games. Some archery events had been held in the 1900, 1904, 1908, and 1920 Olympics, but the competitors were almost entirely from the host nations. In the 1984 Los Angeles games, the archery competition featured the first paraplegic Olympian, who competed in a wheelchair.

THE BIBLE OLYMPIAD

In the Olympics, the archers who most consistently and accurately hit the target win medals.

Here in the Bible Olympiad, we're sorry to say, you *are* the target. You'll win by avoiding the "fiery darts" (Ephesians 6:16) Satan slings your way. Scripture is filled with words of wisdom, encouragement, and example on how to prevail in this challenge. The next competition will test your knowledge of these vital passages.

In the semifinal round, you'll aim to Finish the Verse for a possible 9 points. Then, in the final round, you'll face Multiple Choice and Q & A for potentially 15 more points. As always, you need at least 18 total points (a 75% score) to earn the gold medal. Ready, aim. . .

SEMIFINAL ROUND

1. Neither yield ye your members as _____ of unrighteousness unto sin: but yield yourselves unto God.

2. There hath no temptation taken you but such as is _____ to man.

3. Your adversary, the devil. . .whom _____ stedfast in the faith.

4. Let no man say when he is tempted, I am tempted of _____.

5. After this manner therefore pray ye: . . .lead us not into temptation, but _____ us from evil.

6. In that [Jesus] himself hath _____ being tempted, he is able to succour [help] them that are tempted.

7. The Lord knoweth how to deliver the _____ out of temptations.

8. My son, if sinners _____ thee, consent thou not.

9. Resist the devil, and he will _____ from you.

Answers on page 242.

Score for Semifinal Round: _____
   (1 point per correct answer)

FINAL ROUND

1. What phrase, according to Matthew's Gospel, did Jesus repeat three times while battling Satan's temptation in the wilderness?
   a) "Thou shalt not"
   b) "Get thee behind me"
   c) "Woe unto ye"
   d) "It is written"

2. How many days had Jesus fasted in the wilderness before Satan's temptations began?

3. Who ministered to Jesus after His temptation in the wilderness?

4. What, according to Jesus, is Satan's relationship to lies?
   a) "the father of"
   b) "the creator of"
   c) "the king of"
   d) "the teacher of"

5. What did the apostle Paul tell Timothy to do when tempted by "youthful lusts"?

6. What Old Testament man literally ran from the temptation of the wife of his master, Potiphar?
    a) Joshua
    b) Isaiah
    c) Joseph
    d) Moses

7. What three-letter word describes the distance the wise father in Proverbs told his son to keep from a "strange," or adulterous, woman?

8. What, according to James, is the source of every man's temptation?

9. What did a sorcerer named Simon try to get from Peter by way of a bribe—which the apostle firmly refused?
    a) Jesus' burial cloths
    b) healing from leprosy
    c) the Holy Spirit
    d) a curse on the Jews

10. What desire did Paul warn Timothy about, saying it caused people to "fall into temptation and a snare, and into many foolish and hurtful lusts"?

11. What prophet resisted the temptation to accept money for healing the leper Naaman—then condemned his own servant to leprosy for taking Naaman's money dishonestly?
    a) Samuel
    b) Elijah
    c) Elisha
    d) Obadiah

> OLYMPIC TRIVIA
> *The backyard game of badminton became an Olympic sport in the 1992 games in Barcelona, Spain.*

12. What group of people, described as wolves in sheep's clothing, did Jesus warn His followers to beware of?

13. Whose foolish advice, "Curse God and die," did the righteous, suffering Job resist?
    a) Bildad's
    b) Eliphaz's
    c) Zophar's
    d) his wife's

14. What special "outfit," according to the book of Ephesians, will enable Christians to "withstand in the evil day"?

15. What two words of command did Jesus give His disciples, "lest ye enter into temptation"?

Answers on pages 242–243.

Score for Final Round: _____

(1 point per correct answer)

Combined score for ARCHERY: _____

Points Required for Medals

Gold 18+   Silver 12–17   Bronze 6–11

RANKING: _____

GOOD SPORTS

Good Sport: Bill Havens, U.S.A.
Site: Paris, France
Date: July 17, 1924
Event: Men's Eight-Oared Shell with Coxswain

Bill Havens wasn't actually in Paris, France, for the rowing event called the eight-oared shell with coxswain. The Yale University man could have been—but he chose to stay home with his expectant wife.

Using a replacement for Havens, the nine-man American team brought home the gold, outpacing the silver medalist Canadians and the third place Italians.

Though his concern for his family caused Havens to miss his own chance at Olympic glory, that's not the end of the story. Havens's son, Frank, born just days after the 1924 Olympics ended, grew up to be a rower himself—and won a gold medal in the 1956 Canadian singles 10,000-meter canoeing competition. Frank wired his father from Helsinki, saying, "I'm coming home with the gold medal you should've won."

SKIING

(Backsliding)

Return, ye backsliding children,
and I will heal your backslidings.

JEREMIAH 3:22

COMPETITION
KEYWORDS

Pride

Forsaken

Restore

THE OLYMPIC GAMES

Skiing events have been part of the Olympics since the very first winter games—in Chamonix, France, in 1924. Olympic skiers compete in several "disciplines," including alpine, freestyle, ski jumping, and cross-country.

Alpine events feature the high-speed downhill race and the twisting courses of the slalom, giant slalom, and super giant slalom. Freestyle, developed in the United States in the 1960s, combines elements of alpine skiing with acrobatics, as competitors jump, flip, and spin through the air. Traditional ski jumping, on the other hand, is done for distance. Cross-country skiing tests the endurance of Olympians, who must propel themselves over courses ranging in length from approximately one to thirty-one miles. The "Nordic combined" events involve traditional ski jumping and cross-country races, testing athletes' strength, control, and endurance.

Snowboarding, in which athletes ride a single, wider "ski," has appeared in more recent Olympic games.

THE BIBLE OLYMPIAD

In many Olympic skiing events, the goal is to slide downhill—the faster the better.

Here in the Bible Olympiad, that downhill tendency can get you in trouble. "Backsliding" is the Scriptural term for falling away from the truth—and that's an experience to be avoided at all costs. The Bible is full of warnings against backsliding and, unfortunately, plenty of examples of people who did it. This competition will test your knowledge of these important passages.

In the first event, you'll slalom through 9 turns of Finish the Verse. Next, you'll compete in the "Nordic combined"—featuring Q & A and Multiple Choice questions worth another 15 points. As always, you'll need at least 18 total points (a 75% score) to win gold. Now step up to the starting gate. . . .

SLALOM

1. Jesus said unto him, No man, having put his hand to the _____, and looking back, is fit for the kingdom of God.

2. I have somewhat against thee, because thou hast left thy first _____.

3. Pride goeth before destruction, and an _____ spirit before a fall.

4. Your iniquities have separated between you and your God, and your sins have hid his face from you, that he will not _____.

5. _____ unto me, and I will _____ unto you, saith the LORD of hosts. (Same word, both times.)

6. And the Lord said, Simon, Simon, behold, Satan hath desired to have you, that he may sift you as wheat: But I have prayed for thee, that thy faith fail not: and when thou art converted [when you have turned back], _____ thy brethren.

7. Whereto we have already _____, let us walk by the same rule.

8. Stand fast therefore in the liberty wherewith Christ hath made us free, and be not entangled again with the _____ of bondage

9. How shall we escape, if we neglect so great _____?

Answers on pages 243–244.

Score for Slalom: _____

    (1 point per correct answer)

NORDIC COMBINED

1. What idol did the backsliding Israelites create when Moses was long in returning from his meeting with God on Mount Sinai?

2. What does the Bible say turned Solomon's heart from God during the latter years of his life?
   a) extreme wealth
   b) foreign wives
   c) military successes
   d) human philosophy

3. What Old Testament prophet had to buy back his adulterous wife with silver and barley?

4. What was the name of the above-mentioned prophet's wife?
   a) Abigail
   b) Gomer
   c) Tamar
   d) Tryphena

5. What man, the husband of the beautiful Bathsheba, did King David have killed in a particularly flagrant act of backsliding?

6. What did a sorrowful David later ask God to "restore unto me"?

7. What fellow worker did the apostle Paul say "hath forsaken me, having loved this present world"?
   a) Demas
   b) Tychicus
   c) Luke
   d) Epaphroditus

8. Where did Lot, apparently unwilling to move too far from the soon-to-be-destroyed Sodom, beg God's angels to let him live?
   a) Gaza
   b) Haran
   c) Ur
   d) Zoar

9. In Jesus' parable of the sower, where did the seeds fall that "receive the word with joy; and these have no root, which for a while believe, and in time of temptation fall away"?

GOOD SPORTS

Good Sport: Wilma Rudolph, U.S.A.
Site: Rome, Italy
Date: September 2, 1960
Event: Women's 100 Meters

Born the *twentieth* child of her father (two more siblings would come later), Wilma Rudolph faced a number of physical challenges. She was a premature baby who later contracted scarlet fever, double pneumonia, and polio. From the age of six, she had to wear a brace on her useless left leg.

Her large family proved helpful when a doctor suggested regular rubdowns to stimulate Wilma's bad leg. Four times a day, her mother, brothers, and sisters joined in, and by age eleven, Wilma had thrown off her brace. Soon she was running with blazing speed and earned a spot on the U.S. Olympic team.

Wilma Rudolph was part of the third-place 4 x 100 meter relay team in the 1956 Melbourne games, then dominated the field in the 1960 Rome Olympics. Her 100-meter time of 11.0 seconds was three-tenths of a second better than the silver medalist, and she won other gold medals in the 200 meters and the 4 x 100 relay.

WRESTLING

(Spiritual Struggles)

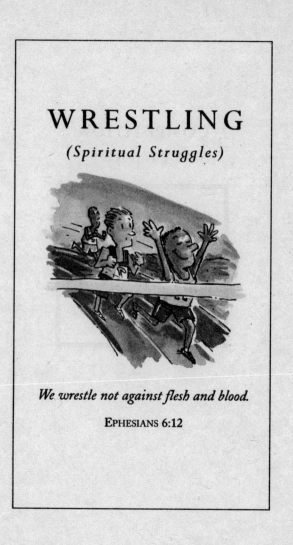

We wrestle not against flesh and blood.

EPHESIANS 6:12

COMPETITION
KEYWORDS

Strive

Trial

Power

THE OLYMPIC GAMES

Olympic wrestling matches occur in two separate disciplines: freestyle and Greco-Roman.

Greco-Roman wrestling was invented in France in the 1800s and named for the ancient cultures that contributed so much to modern sports. A "super heavyweight" match was held in the first modern Olympics, in Athens, Greece, in 1896. Freestyle matches began appearing in the 1904 games in St. Louis.

Wrestlers in each discipline earn points for "holds" they put on their opponents and for other actions such as causing an opponent to lose all contact with the ground. Competitors win matches by having the most points at the end of a timed round, by achieving a lead of ten points, or by causing a "fall"—holding an opponent so that both of his shoulders are touching the mat.

Wrestlers compete in several different weight classes, ranging from flyweight (a maximum of 119 pounds) to super heavyweight (a maximum of 286 pounds). Unlike the other Olympic sports, wrestling does have an upper weight limit for its athletes.

THE BIBLE OLYMPIAD

Olympic wrestlers struggle for position, leverage, and any other advantage they can gain over their opponents.

Here in the Bible Olympiad, you'll face a similar struggle—as your opponent, Satan, tries to gain the upper hand on you. The Scriptures are clear about the struggles this life will bring and the methods you can use to neutralize them. This competition will test your knowledge of these very important passages.

In the semifinal match, you'll wrestle against Finish the Verse for a possible 9 points. In the finals, you'll be pitted against Q & A and Multiple Choice worth another potential 15 points. As with every Bible Olympiad contest, you'll need at least 18 points (a 75% score) to earn the gold. Take your positions!

SEMIFINAL MATCH

1. Ye have not yet resisted unto _____, striving against sin.

2. Whereunto I also _____, striving according to his working, which worketh in me mightily.

3. To be carnally minded is death; but to be spiritually minded is life and _____.

4. Let us not therefore judge one another any more: but judge this rather, that no man put a _____ or an occasion to fall in his brother's way.

5. Let not the sun go down upon your wrath: Neither give place to the _____.

6. Neither be partaker of other men's _____: keep thyself pure.

7. Who shall _____ us from the love of Christ? shall tribulation, or distress, or persecution, or famine, or nakedness, or peril, or sword?

8. The _____ of our warfare are not carnal, but mighty through God to the pulling down of strong holds.

9. Finally, my brethren, be _____ in the Lord, and in the power of his might.

Answers on page 245.

Score for Semifinal Match: _____

    (1 point per correct answer)

FINALS

1. What Old Testament character literally wrestled with God?
   a) Noah
   b) Jacob
   c) Enoch
   d) David

2. What was it, according to the apostle Paul, that "dwelleth in me" and caused him to struggle spiritually?
   a) evil
   b) carnality
   c) falsehood
   d) sin

3. According to the three-part warning in the Book of James, "when lust hath conceived, it bringeth forth sin: and sin, when it is finished, bringeth forth" *what*?

4. What, according to James, is enmity, or hatred, toward God?

5. What did the apostle Paul tell the Corinthians "evil communications" (or "bad company" in the NIV) will do to good manners or morals?
   a) assault
   b) besmirch
   c) corrupt
   d) destroy

6. What did Paul write to the Corinthians that "we are not ignorant of" regarding Satan?

7. According to the apostle Paul, what kind of angel can Satan masquerade as?

8. What did Peter tell Christians to "think it not" concerning the "fiery trial which is to try you"?
   a) strange
   b) frightening
   c) sad
   d) uncommon

9. What does James say to "count it all" when faced by "divers temptations," or "trials of many kinds" (NIV)?

10. What prophet went into depression when the evil Queen Jezebel threatened his life?
   a) Isaiah
   b) Nathan
   c) Samuel
   d) Elijah

> **OLYMPIC TRIVIA**
> *Uljana Semjonova helped the Soviet Union win gold medals in women's basketball in both the 1976 Montreal and 1980 Moscow Olympics. She was 6'10½" tall and weighed more than 280 pounds.*

11. What disciple of Jesus apparently had to overcome a negative disposition—as expressed at the death of Lazarus and the resurrection of Christ?
   a) Matthew
   b) Thomas
   c) Bartholomew
   d) Andrew

12. What does the Book of 1 Corinthians say will test what Christians have built on Christ's foundation—whether they've used "gold, silver, precious stones, wood, hay, [or] stubble"?

13. What type of fruit, according to the Book of Hebrews, is grown in the Christian's life through chastening, or discipline?

14. What two-word phrase, part of the title of a classic Christian novel, describes the example of the suffering Jesus that believers should follow?

15. What "S" word, meaning "to yield," does James urge Christians to do to God?

Answers on pages 245–246.

Score for Finals: _____

(1 point per correct answer)

Combined score for WRESTLING: _____

Points Required for Medals

Gold 18+   Silver 12–17   Bronze 6–11

RANKING: _____

GOOD SPORTS

Good Sport: Henry Pearce, Australia
Site: Amsterdam, Netherlands
Date: August 10, 1928
Event: Men's Single Sculls

Sculling is a type of rowing race, and Australian Henry "Bobby" Pearce won the gold medal in the 2,000-meter race (about one and a quarter miles) in 1928. What makes him a good sport is the considerate treatment he showed to others in the water in his quarterfinal contest.

The "others" in this case were *ducks*—Pearce actually stopped rowing in the middle of his race to allow a family of ducks to swim across his path. When the birds were safely out of his way, he resumed his rowing and still defeated his quarterfinal opponent. Pearce later went on to win the gold medal.

In the 1932 Los Angeles Olympics, Pearce earned another gold medal for Australia—though, this time, there were no feathered obstacles to slow his progress.

HURDLES

(Overcoming)

Be of good cheer;
I have overcome the world.

<small>JOHN 16:33</small>

COMPETITION
KEYWORDS

Overcome

Strength

Victory

THE OLYMPIC GAMES

To "hurdle" means "to leap over, especially while running"—so the hurdles competition is a footrace with obstacles to be jumped.

Both men and women compete in Olympic hurdles races. The men's 110-meter event dates back to the first modern Olympics in Athens, Greece, in 1896, while a 400-meter race was added to the 1900 games in Paris. Women also run a 400-meter race, which first appeared in the 1984 Los Angeles games, but their shorter race is only 100 meters. It debuted at the 1932 Olympics, also held in Los Angeles.

In all four races, runners must clear ten hurdles, spaced at equal distances throughout the course. In the men's 110-meter race, the hurdles are 3½ feet high; in the 400-meter race, they're 3 feet tall. The women's hurdles are slightly lower: 2 feet 9 inches in the 100-meter race and 2 feet 6 inches in the 400 meters.

THE BIBLE OLYMPIAD

To reach the finish line, hurdlers must be over-comers—able to leap all the obstacles that confront them on the track.

Here in the Bible Olympiad, you'll need a similar ability—the ability to overcome life's challenges. The good news is that you'll have God's help to do that. . . and the pages of Scripture are filled with words of advice and encouragement. This competition will test your knowledge of those key passages.

In the preliminary heat, you'll face the 9 hurdles of Finish the Verse. In the finals, you'll need to leap 15 hurdles of Q & A and Multiple Choice. As in every competition, you'll need at least 18 total points (a 75% score) to take home the gold. On your mark. . .

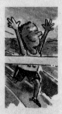

PRELIMINARY HEAT

1. Be not overcome of _____.

2. I have written unto you, young men, because ye are strong, and the _____ _____ _____ abideth in you, and ye have overcome the wicked one.

3. Ye are of God, little children, and have overcome them: because _____ is he that is in you, than he that is in the world.

4. Whatsoever is born of God overcometh the world: and this is the victory that overcometh the world, even our _____.

5. Him that overcometh will I make a _____ in the temple of my God.

6. To him that overcometh will I give to eat of the tree of _____, which is in the midst of the paradise of God.

7. He that overcometh shall _____ all things; and I will be his God, and he shall be my son.

8. Who is he that overcometh the world, but he that believeth that Jesus is the _____ _____ _____?

9. To him that overcometh will I grant to sit with me in my _____.

Answers on page 246.

Score for Preliminary Heat: _____

    (1 point per correct answer)

FINALS

1. What does the book of Philippians say believers can do "through Christ which strengtheneth me"?
   - a) all things
   - b) miracles
   - c) good deeds
   - d) acts of mercy

2. What two-word phrase of the apostle Paul described to the Ephesians what God is able to do "above all that we ask or think"?

3. What "S" word did God promise to Joshua if "this book of the law shall not depart out of thy mouth; but thou shalt meditate therein day and night, that thou mayest observe to do according to all that is written therein"?

4. What Old Testament leader overcame a huge enemy army, "like grasshoppers for multitude," with three hundred men handpicked by God Himself?
   - a) Samson
   - b) Gideon
   - c) David
   - d) Saul

5. What Old Testament prophet's faithfulness to God overcame the jealous plots of fellow government officials—so that he "prospered in the reign of Darius, and in the reign of Cyrus the Persian"?
   a) Isaiah
   b) Jeremiah
   c) Daniel
   d) Ezekiel

6. What did God do to "the latter end of Job more than his beginning," after Job's faithful perseverance through Satan's attacks?

7. How old was Joseph when, after years of imprisonment on false charges, he rose to become second-in-command of Egypt?
   a) 18 years old
   b) 30 years old
   c) 50 years old
   d) 90 years old

8. What completes Joseph's comment to the brothers who had sold him into slavery years before: "Ye thought evil against me. . ."?

9. When Jesus sent out seventy disciples with authority over "all the power of the enemy," what venomous creatures did He tell them "I give you power to tread on"?

10. What did Jesus tell His seventy disciples to rejoice in—beyond the physical and spiritual protection mentioned in the preceding question?
    a) "your names are written in heaven"
    b) "the Christ is given for men"
    c) "Satan's doom is sure"
    d) "the Father loveth his children"

11. What part of the body did Jesus tell His disciples to "offer also" to "him that smiteth thee on the one"?

> **OLYMPIC TRIVIA**
> *American gymnast George Eyser won six medals—three gold, two silver, and a bronze—at the 1904 St. Louis Olympics, competing on a wooden leg.*

12. What did Paul command the Thessalonians not to "render," or pay back, "unto any man"?

13. When Jesus commanded "love ye your enemies, and do good, and lend, hoping for nothing again," what was He urging His disciples to be "as your Father also is"?
    a) wise
    b) loving
    c) longsuffering
    d) merciful

14. When the apostle Paul wrote, "O death, where is thy sting? O grave, where is thy victory?" what did he say that God "giveth us the victory through"?

15. What does the apostle Paul say Christians are "more than. . .through him that loved us"?

Answers on pages 246–247.

Score for Finals: _____
   (1 point per correct answer)

Combined score for HURDLES: _____

Points Required for Medals

Gold 18+   Silver 12–17   Bronze 6–11

RANKING: _____

GOOD SPORTS

Good Sport: Bill Roycroft, Australia
Site: Rome, Italy
Date: September 10, 1960
Event: Equestrian Three-Day Team Event

Australian horseman Bill Roycroft couldn't let his team down—not even while he was recuperating from a concussion and broken collarbone suffered in a fall.

The forty-five year old equestrian left his hospital bed to compete in the 1960 jumping test. Without his participation, Roycroft's two teammates would have lost their chance at a gold medal. With his efforts, Australia earned its first top finish in forty-eight years of the team competition.

Roycroft's tenacity was further demonstrated by his participation in the next *four* Olympic games. Three of his sons also joined him on Australia's Olympic teams.

BALANCE BEAM

(*Priorities*)

Seek ye first the kingdom of God,
and his righteousness.

MATTHEW 6:33

COMPETITION
KEYWORDS

First

Greatest

Holy

THE OLYMPIC GAMES

The balance beam, part of the Olympic gymnastics competition, is contested only on the women's program.

The beam itself is approximately 16 feet long and 4 inches wide and stands almost 4 feet above the floor. Competitors perform a routine of 70 to 90 seconds, exhibiting balance, strength, and artistry. Jumps, handstands, and cartwheels can all be part of the routine.

The balance beam competition first appeared in the 1952 Helsinki games and has featured some of the biggest names in Olympic history: the Soviet Olga Korbut in the 1972 Munich and 1976 Montreal games, the Romanian Nadia Comaneci in the 1976 Montreal and 1980 Moscow games, and the American Mary Lou Retton in the 1984 Los Angeles games. In the 1996 Atlanta games, Shannon Miller's first place finish made her the first American gold medalist in the event.

THE BIBLE OLYMPIAD

Olympic gymnasts must display perfect equilibrium to succeed in the balance beam competition.

Here in the Bible Olympiad, balance is key to success, as well—but this balance relates to the priorities of life. The Bible offers much advice on setting the proper priorities and finding the balance that God desires, often by emphasizing the word "first." This competition will test your knowledge of these important passages.

You'll open with a Finish the Verse qualifying routine worth a possible 9 points. After that, the championship routine, consisting of Q & A and Multiple Choice questions, could add 15 more points to your total. This competition, like the others, requires a total of at least 18 points (a 75% score) for a gold-medal finish. Up to the beam!

QUALIFYING ROUTINE

1. I delivered unto you first of all that which I also received, how that Christ died for our sins according to the _____.

2. The gospel must first be published among all _____.

3. I exhort therefore, that, first of all, supplications, prayers, intercessions, and giving of thanks, be made for _____ men.

4. If thou bring thy gift to the altar, and there rememberest that thy brother hath ought against thee; leave there thy gift before the altar, and go thy way; first be _____ to thy brother.

5. How wilt thou say to thy brother, Let me pull out the mote out of thine eye; and, behold, a beam is in thine own eye? Thou _____, first cast out the beam out of thine own eye.

6. Which of you, intending to build a tower, sitteth not down first, and counteth the _____, whether he have sufficient to finish it?

7. If any man desire to be first, the same shall be last of all, and _____ of all.

8. [Jesus] is the head of the body, the church: who is the beginning, the _____ from the dead; that in all things he might have the preeminence.

9. The Lord himself shall descend from heaven with a shout, with the voice of the archangel, and with the trump of God: and the _____ _____ _____ shall rise first.

Answers on pages 247–248.

Score for Qualifying Routine: _____

    (1 point per correct answer)

CHAMPIONSHIP ROUTINE

1. What did Jesus say was the "first and great commandment"?

2. What does the apostle Paul call the "first commandment with promise"?

3. Of what key quality did the writer of Hebrews say, "without which no man shall see the Lord"?
   a) love
   b) patience
   c) mercy
   d) holiness

4. What, according to Proverbs, is "the principal thing," or "supreme" as the New International Version says?
   a) wisdom
   b) wealth
   c) love
   d) longevity

5. What Old Testament prophet urged a widow of Zarephath to use her meager supply of oil and flour to feed him first—promising that if she did, God would supply her food until a drought had passed?

6. When does the apostle Paul urge Christians to set aside money for the Lord's offering?

7. Where did poverty-stricken believers "first [give] their own selves to the Lord, and unto us by the will of God," and donate generously to the apostle Paul's ministry?
   a) Macedonia
   b) Mamre
   c) Megiddo
   d) Midian

8. Who, according to Paul, is to have first responsibility for caring for a widow in the church?
   a) the widow herself
   b) her children and other relatives
   c) the church
   d) the government

9. How did a wealthy young man feel after Jesus told him to sell his possessions and give everything to the poor?

10. What command, also a favorite of John the Baptist, did the apostle Paul say he "shewed first unto them of Damascus, and at Jerusalem, and throughout all the coasts of Judea"?

11. What completes the apostle Paul's introduction to his letter to the Christians in Rome: "First, I. . ."?
    a) "encourage hospitality"
    b) "commend your faith"
    c) "reject your error"
    d) "thank my God"

12. In what city did Jesus' disciples first take the name "Christians"?

13. What disciple, upon following Jesus, "first findeth his own brother Simon, and saith unto him, We have found the Messias"?
    a) James
    b) Matthew
    c) Andrew
    d) Nathanael

> OLYMPIC TRIVIA
> *The Olympics' oldest competitor— and medalist— is Oscar Swahn of Sweden. He was nearing 73 years of age when he earned a bronze medal in a shooting competition at the 1920 Antwerp Olympics.*

14. What man is commended in Hebrews for "choosing rather to suffer affliction with the people of God, than to enjoy the pleasures of sin for a season"?

15. What "more excellent way" does the apostle Paul urge Christians to follow in 1 Corinthians 13?

Answers on page 248.

Score for Championship Routine: _____
  (1 point per correct answer)

Combined score for BALANCE BEAM: _____

Points Required for Medals

Gold 18+   Silver 12–17   Bronze 6–11

RANKING: _____

GOOD SPORTS

Good Sport: Micheline Ostermeyer, France
Site: London, England
Date: August 4, 1948
Event: Women's Shot Put and Discus

Many Olympic athletes begin playing their sports at very young ages. Some observers worry that "sport is life" for too many athletes—that those who participate in the highest level of the game may somehow have missed out on other important aspects of living.

French track and field star Micheline Ostermeyer might argue that point. She took gold medals in both the shot put and discus competitions at the 1948 London Olympics, adding a bronze medal in the high jump, as well. Only weeks before the Olympics began, she had graduated with high honors from the Paris Conservatory of Music as a concert pianist.

Ostermeyer believed that her involvement in sports helped her music, and vice versa. "Sport taught me to relax," she said. "The piano gave me strong biceps."

HIGH JUMP

(Striving for Excellence)

*Whatever happens,
conduct yourselves in a manner
worthy of the gospel of Christ.*

PHILIPPIANS 1:27 NIV

COMPETITION
KEYWORDS

Whatsoever

Excellent

Follow

THE OLYMPIC GAMES

The Olympic high jump is a pretty straightforward competition—athletes vie to see who can jump highest over a measured bar.

Men's high jump was part of the track and field competition at the first modern Olympics in Athens, Greece, in 1896. Women first took part in the 1928 Amsterdam games. Athletes sprint along an 82-foot runway before propelling themselves upward, off one foot, toward a 13-foot long crossbar. A successful jump is one in which the competitor goes over the bar without knocking it off its supports. The bar may be touched, as long as it doesn't fall.

High jumpers may begin jumping at any height and may pass at any height, but three consecutive misses result in elimination. When ties occur, the competitor who had the fewest misses at the last cleared height is declared the winner.

THE BIBLE OLYMPIAD

Olympic high jumpers defy gravity to see who can propel their bodies the farthest upward.

Here in the Bible Olympiad, you'll always strive for greater heights, too—greater heights of spiritual commitment, that is. The Bible is filled with verses that encourage a striving for excellence in everything we do. This competition will test your knowledge of these challenging passages.

In your first jump, you'll attempt to clear the 9-point Finish the Verse level. Then the bar rises—to the 15-point level of Q & A and Multiple Choice questions. As in every competition at the Bible Olympiad, you need at least 18 total points (a 75% score) to win the gold medal. When I say "jump. . ."

FIRST JUMP

1. Whether therefore ye eat, or drink, or whatsoever ye do, do all to the _____ of God.

2. Looking unto Jesus the _____ and finisher of our faith. . . .

3. Whatsoever ye do in word or deed, do all in the name of the Lord Jesus, giving _____ to God and the Father by him.

4. See that none render evil for evil unto any man; but ever follow that which is _____, both among yourselves, and to all men.

5. Whatsoever ye do, do it _____, as to the Lord, and not unto men.

6. But thou, O _____ _____ _____. . . follow after righteousness, godliness, faith, love, patience, meekness.

7. It is written, Be ye _____; for I am _____. (Same word, both times.)

8. Be ye therefore followers of God, as dear children; and walk in _____.

9. And this I pray, that your love may _____ yet more and more in knowledge and in all judgment; that ye may approve things that are excellent.

Answers on page 249.

Score for First Jump: _____
     (1 point per correct answer)

FINAL JUMP

1. What personified quality in the Book of
   Proverbs says, "Hear; for I will speak of excellent
   (or worthy) things"?
   - a) wisdom
   - b) mercy
   - c) hope
   - d) peace

2. What did Paul tell the Philippians to do with
   "whatsoever things are true. . .honest. . .just. . .
   pure. . .lovely. . .of good report"?

3. What two-word phrase did the apostle Paul tell
   the Colossians to set their affections on?

4. What did the psalm writer say to "seek. . .and
   pursue it"?
   - a) love
   - b) joy
   - c) peace
   - d) patience

5. According to the apostle Paul's letter to the Ephesians, what are Christians to "walk as children of"?

6. What word, according to Jesus, describes the way or road "which leadeth unto life"?

7. What type of sacrifice did the apostle Paul tell the Romans to "present your bodies" to God?
   a) perfect
   b) daily
   c) living
   d) sinless

8. What strong verb did the apostle Paul use to describe his efforts to reach "the mark for the prize of the high calling of God in Christ Jesus"?

9. Who is quoted in the Bible as saying "We ought to obey God rather than men"?
   a) Abraham
   b) Noah
   c) Jonah
   d) Peter

10. What "eloquent man. . .mighty in the scriptures," was willing to accept the teaching of Aquila and Priscilla, who "expounded unto him the way of God more perfectly"?
    a) Luke
    b) Barnabas
    c) Titus
    d) Apollos

> OLYMPIC TRIVIA
> *U.S. swimmer Michael Barrowman's neighbors celebrated his first-place finish in the 200-meter breaststroke at the 1992 Barcelona Olympics by covering his front lawn with gold paint.*

11. What two Israelite spies were commended for the way they "wholly followed the LORD"—as opposed to ten other spies who gave a bad report on the land of Canaan?

12. What did Daniel say he wouldn't do with the king of Babylon's meat and wine?
    a) imperil himself
    b) satisfy himself
    c) defile himself
    d) burden himself

13. What did Paul tell the Corinthians he "put away" when he became a man?

14. What did the apostle Paul consider everything he had lost for the sake of Jesus Christ?

15. What four things did Jesus say "thou shalt love the Lord thy God with all thy"?

Answers on pages 249–250.

Score for Final Jump: _____

(1 point per correct answer)

Combined score for HIGH JUMP: _____

Points Required for Medals

Gold 18+   Silver 12–17   Bronze 6–11

RANKING: _____

GOOD SPORTS

Good Sport: Neroli Fairhall, New Zealand
Site: Los Angeles, California
Date: August 11, 1984
Event: Women's Archery

A thirty-fifth place finish is not what most Olympic athletes dream of. But for Neroli Fairhall of New Zealand, it was quite an accomplishment.

Fairhall, competing in the women's archery contest at the 1984 Los Angeles games, became the first paraplegic athlete to participate in the Olympics. She shot her bow while sitting in a wheelchair, having lost the use of her legs in a cycling accident.

Twelve years later, in Atlanta, Georgia, Italian archer Paola Fantato became the second wheelchair-using competitor in Olympic history. She placed in fifty-fourth position.

MARATHON

(Endurance)

*Run in such a way
as to get the prize.*

1 CORINTHIANS 9:24 NIV

COMPETITION
KEYWORDS

Abide

Endure

Patience

THE OLYMPIC GAMES

The marathon is the Olympics' ultimate test of endurance. Organizers devised the race around the legend of an ancient Greek messenger who ran more than twenty miles carrying news of the battle of Marathon—and then died immediately after telling of victory.

The men's marathon dates back to the very first "modern" Olympic games, in Athens in 1896. It would be another 88 years before women would compete in an Olympic marathon in the 1984 Los Angeles games.

Modern marathon runners cover a course that is 26 miles, 385 yards long. The odd length originated at the 1908 London Olympics, when English sporting officials arranged the race to begin at Windsor Castle and end in front of the queen's box in London's White City Stadium.

Competitors may stop at official "refreshment stations" set up every 3.1 miles along the course, and at water stations in between, but are disqualified if they receive any other outside assistance. Olympic marathoners, male or female, complete the course in less than two and a half hours.

THE BIBLE OLYMPIAD

Endurance—the ability to stick with something long-term—is the name of the game in marathon running.

Here in the Bible Olympiad, endurance will spell the difference between your breaking the tape with energy and flair or your limping and stumbling across the finish line. You'll want a strong performance over the entire, long-distance Christian life, to propel you toward the best reward. The Bible gives plenty of instruction on enduring and examples of those who did and didn't endure well. The next competition will test your knowledge of those passages.

In the warm-up, you'll try to be first to Finish the Verse—with a possible 9 points at stake. In the actual marathon to follow, you'll run up against Q & A and Multiple Choice questions worth an additional 15 points. Remember that you need at least 18 total points (a 75% score) to win the gold medal. Take your mark!

WARM-UP

1. Let us run with _____ the race that is set before us.

2. I have finished my course, I have kept the _____.

3. Let us not be _____ in well doing: for in due season we shall reap, if we faint not.

4. As the Father hath loved me, so have I loved you: _____ ye in my love.

5. Exhorting them to continue in the faith, and that we must through much _____ enter into the kingdom of God.

6. Then said Jesus to those Jews which believed on him, If you continue in my word, then are ye my _____ indeed.

7. Abide in me, and I in you. As the branch cannot bear fruit of itself, except it abide in the _____; no more can ye, except ye abide in me.

8. If ye endure chastening, God dealeth with you as with _____.

9. But he that shall endure unto the end, the same shall be _____.

Answers on page 250.

Score for Warm-Up: _____

(1 point per correct answer)

MARATHON

1. What, according to the book of Hebrews, did Jesus endure "for the joy that was set before him"?

2. Which church of Asia Minor, to which the apostle Paul wrote a letter, did Jesus commend in Revelation for its "patience," or "perseverance" (NIV)?

3. How did Paul tell Timothy to "endure hardness"?
    a) "as a runner"
    b) "as a good soldier"
    c) "as a mighty oak"
    d) "as a stone"

4. Which of the following is *not* a hardship the apostle Paul had to endure, according to his list in 2 Corinthians 11?
    a) shipwreck
    b) beatings
    c) wild animals
    d) robbers

5. How many people accepted the gospel message at Pentecost, then "continued stedfastly" in the apostles' teaching, fellowship, communion, and prayer?
   a) 12
   b) 150
   c) 3,000
   d) 10,000

6. How many men were chosen to "serve tables" while the twelve apostles devoted themselves "continually to prayer, and to the ministry of the word"?

7. What, according to Paul's first letter to the Corinthians, are Christians to "stand fast" in?

8. What country did Joseph, the faithful slave who remained true to God, eventually rise to rule?

9. Where was Joseph when the king, wanting the interpretation of a dream, called for him?
   a) in a dungeon
   b) in the army
   c) in Potiphar's house
   d) in the temple

10. What successor to Moses was told by God to observe the law and "turn not from it to the right hand or to the left"?

11. What construction project did Nehemiah bring to a successful conclusion despite the mocking and threats of enemies?
    a) the tower of David
    b) the temple
    c) King Solomon's palace
    d) the wall of Jerusalem

12. What did each of Nehemiah's workers keep by his side during the construction?
    a) a lamp
    b) water
    c) a sword
    d) Scripture

13. What Old Testament character was noted by the New Testament writer James for his "patience," or "perseverance" (NIV)?

> **OLYMPIC TRIVIA**
> *The modern pentathlon is a military-oriented competition featuring horse riding, running, swimming, fencing, and pistol shooting. In the 1912 Stockholm Olympics, the United States' top finisher was future World War II general George Patton.*

14. What, according to James, "worketh patience," or "perseverance" (NIV), in the Christian's life?

15. What two things, according to Ephesians 6:10, are Christians to "be strong in"?

Answers on pages 250–251.

Score for Marathon: _____
   (1 point per correct answer)

Combined score for MARATHON: _____

Points Required for Medals

Gold 18+   Silver 12–17   Bronze 6–11

RANKING: _____

GOOD SPORTS

Good Sport: David Albritton, U.S.A.
Site: Berlin, Germany
Date: August 2, 1936
Event: Men's High Jump

In the racially charged atmosphere of the 1936 Berlin Olympics, David Albritton was one of several black Americans to disprove Adolf Hitler's belief in "Aryan superiority."

Albritton and fellow black American Cornelius Johnson took the silver and gold, respectively, in the high jump competition. Then they were snubbed by Hitler, who had personally congratulated German and Finnish athletes in earlier ceremonies, but left the stadium before the high jump awards.

Returning to an America still coming to terms with racial equality, Albritton became a high school teacher and coach, motivating hundreds of students to pursue their education. He also served more than a decade in the state legislature of Ohio.

THE CLOSING CEREMONY

(Rewards)

*Everyone who competes in the games
goes into strict training. . . .
We do it to get a crown that will last forever.*

1 CORINTHIANS 9:25 NIV

COMPETITION
KEYWORDS

Crown

Reward

Eternal

THE OLYMPIC GAMES

The Olympics bring together many of the best athletes in the entire world—so placing in the top three of a given event is a major accomplishment.

Top finishers in the Olympics are known as "medalists" for the gold, silver, and bronze medals they receive. That tradition began with the St. Louis Olympics of 1904; in prior games, winners had received cups, trophies, diplomas, and crowns made of olive or laurel branches.

For each event, the top placing athletes mount a special podium to receive their respective medals. Many athletes have said that one of the highlights of their Olympic experience is hearing their national anthem played during the awards ceremony.

THE BIBLE OLYMPIAD

It's a tremendous honor to be chosen for a nation's Olympic team. But the competitive nature of athletes compels them to do more than just participate—they each want to win.

Here in the Bible Olympiad, the competition is less against others as it is an internal struggle to do one's best and honor God—who serves as the ultimate judge. The good news is that there can and will be many "winners," and the Bible is filled with verses that promise out-of-this-world rewards for successful participation. As you conclude your time on the Bible Olympiad team, you'll have one final competition to test your knowledge of these key passages.

As you step to the podium, a final round of Finish the Verse, worth 9 points, awaits you. After that, as the national anthem plays, you can earn up to 15 additional points in Multiple Choice and Q & A. If you successfully log 18 points (a 75% score), you can leave the stadium with one final gold medal. *Bon voyage!*

PODIUM

1. There is laid up for me a crown of righteousness, which the Lord, the righteous judge, shall
   give me at that day: and not to me only, but
   unto all them also that love his _____.

2. Blessed is the man that endureth temptation: for
   when he is tried, he shall receive the crown of
   _____, which the Lord hath promised to
   them that love him.

3. They that be wise shall shine as the brightness
   of the firmament; and they that turn many to
   righteousness as the _____ for ever and ever.

4. If we suffer, we shall also _____ with him.

5. We are confident, I say, and willing rather to be
   absent from the body, and to be present with the
   _____.

6. I reckon that the sufferings of this present time
   are not worthy to be compared with the
   _____ which shall be revealed in us.

7. Love ye your enemies, and do good, and lend, hoping for nothing again; and your reward shall be _____.

8. Then shall the _____ shine forth as the sun in the kingdom of their Father.

9. We know that if our earthly house of this tabernacle were dissolved, we have a _____ of God, an house not made with hands, eternal in the heavens.

Answers on pages 251–252.

Score for Podium: _____

(1 point per correct answer)

NATIONAL ANTHEM

1. In one of Jesus' parables, what congratulatory two-word phrase does the master have for his servants who multiplied the talents he gave them?

2. What did the psalm writer David say are at God's right hand "for evermore"?
   a) blessings
   b) victories
   c) pleasures
   d) gifts

3. What two words did James use to describe the gifts that come down "from above. . .from the Father of lights"?

4. What had God, according to the Book of Colossians, "delivered us from" when He "translated us into the kingdom of his dear Son"?
   a) "the power of darkness"
   b) "the fire of hell"
   c) "the pain of suffering"
   d) "the schemes of Satan"

5. Who viewed "the reproach of Christ greater riches than the treasure" of his adopted homeland and was honored in the Hebrews 11 "Faith Hall of Fame"?
   a) Moses
   b) Joseph
   c) Daniel
   d) Ezekiel

6. Where did Jesus tell the believing criminal on the cross beside Him "to day shalt thou be with me"?

7. Where did Jesus say a "great" reward awaits those who persevere when "men shall revile you, and persecute you, and shall say all manner of evil against you falsely, for my sake"?

8. What small gift, given to a believing child, did Jesus say was worthy of a lasting reward?
   a) "a loaf of bread"
   b) "a cup of cold water"
   c) "a cake of figs"
   d) "a word of praise"

9. What special tree is made available to those whose names are "written in the Lamb's book of life"?

10. What two farming terms does the apostle Paul use to explain how Christians obtain "life everlasting" from the Spirit?

11. What did Jesus say "my kingdom is not of"?
    a) the flesh
    b) silver and gold
    c) strife
    d) this world

OLYMPIC TRIVIA
Triple jumper James Connolly of Boston won the first event at the 1896 Athens Olympics—thus becoming the first Olympic champion in 1,527 years.

---

12. What two destroyers, according to Jesus, will never "corrupt" one's treasures in heaven?

13. What verb completes Jesus' comment from the Book of John: "If any man" *what* "me, him will my Father honour"?
    a) honour
    b) serve
    c) love
    d) remember

14. What legal relationship did God choose for his children, allowing Christians to cry, "Abba, Father"?

15. What completes the following quotation from the first letter of John: "And this is the record, that God hath given to us eternal life, and this life is in. . ."?

Answers on page 252.

Score for National Anthem: _____
   (1 point per correct answer)

Combined score for THE CLOSING CEREMONY: _____

Points Required for Medals

Gold 18+   Silver 12–17   Bronze 6–11

RANKING: _____

GOOD SPORTS

Good Sport: Eric Liddell, Great Britain
Site: Paris, France
Date: July 11, 1924
Event: Men's 400 Meters

Not many major motion pictures have profiled a Christian athlete. But not many Christian athletes have a story like Eric Liddell, the hero of *Chariots of Fire*.

He was born in China to missionary parents and soon developed a deep faith of his own. Growing up in Scotland, Eric's running abilities quickly became apparent, and he emerged as one of Scotland's greatest hopes for an Olympic gold medal. But here his faith and his athletic abilities collided—when Liddell learned that heats of his best race, the 100 meters, would be held on a Sunday, his respect for the Lord's Day compelled him to withdraw.

The 400-meter races would not be held on Sundays, though, and Liddell began training for them. In the finals, he ran an unorthodox race, at full speed from start to finish, and set an Olympic record of 47.6 seconds. Liddell returned to Scotland a national hero, but within a year was on the mission field in China.

Twenty years later, caught in the upheaval of World War 2, Liddell died of a brain tumor in a Japanese internment camp. When his unmarked grave was found nearly a half century later, it was noted with a granite monument bearing the words of Isaiah 40:31: "They shall mount up with wings as eagles; they shall run, and not be weary."

ANSWERS

He shall call upon me,
and I will answer him.

PSALM 91:15

TRAINING

Skills Training
1. way (Proverbs 22:6)
2. Lord (Ephesians 6:4)
3. loveth (Hebrews 12:6)
4. ungodliness (Titus 2:11–12)
5. works (2 Timothy 3:16–17)
6. wiser (Proverbs 9:9)
7. spiritual (Colossians 3:16)
8. godliness (1 Timothy 4:7)
9. trembling (Philippians 2:12)

Endurance Training
1. c) an incorruptible crown (1 Corinthians 9:25)
2. learn (Matthew 11:29)
3. law (Galatians 3:24–25)
4. b) "whatsoever things were written aforetime" (Romans 15:4)
5. d) Moses (Exodus 3:11, 4:12)
6. Isaiah (Isaiah 1:17, 6:1)
7. fear (Deuteronomy 4:10, 14:23, 17:19, 31:12, 31:13)
8. Samuel (1 Samuel 12:23–24)
9. a) "and he shall direct thy paths" (Proverbs 3:6)
10. "Be ye doers," or "Do what it says" (James 1:22)
11. d) "draw nigh to God" (James 4:8)

12. "in season, out of season" (2 Timothy 4:2)
13. a) "to be content" (Philippians 4:11)
14. an answer (1 Peter 3:15)
15. "I am holy" (1 Peter 1:16)

LONG JUMP

Qualifying Round
1. word of God (Romans 10:17)
2. please (Hebrews 11:6)
3. mustard (Matthew 17:20)
4. just (Romans 1:17)
5. peace (Romans 5:1)
6. sight (2 Corinthians 5:7)
7. law (Galatians 2:16)
8. dead (James 2:26)
9. Examine (2 Corinthians 13:5)

Final Round
1. a) Abraham (James 2:23)

2. Abel (Hebrews 11:4)
3. b) eternal life (1 John 5:13)
4. perish (John 3:16)
5. Nebuchadnezzar (Daniel 3:16–30)
6. d) "they were hanged" (Hebrews 11:37)
7. Isaac (Hebrews 11:17–19)
8. a) Enoch (Hebrews 11:5)
9. the Red Sea (Hebrews 11:29)
10. a tempest, or storm (Matthew 8:23–27)
11. b) blindness (Matthew 9:27–30)
12. d) "Repent ye" (Mark 1:15)
13. Rahab (Joshua 2, Hebrews 11:31)
14. works, or action (James 2:17)
15. all things, or everything (Mark 9:23)

FIGURE SKATING

Short Program
1. faith (Ephesians 2:8)
2. throne (Hebrews 4:16)
3. humble (James 4:6)

4. knowledge (2 Peter 3:18)
5. stand (Romans 5:1–2)
6. redemption (Ephesians 1:7)
7. sin (Romans 5:20)
8. I am (1 Corinthians 15:10)
9. justified (Romans 3:24)

Free Skate

1. b) peace (Romans 1:7, 1 Corinthians 1:3, 2 Corinthians 1:2, etc.)
2. sufficient (2 Corinthians 12:9)
3. a "thorn in the flesh" (2 Corinthians 12:7)
4. d) the humble (James 4:6)
5. b) Noah (Genesis 6:8)
6. Jonah (Jonah 4:1–2)
7. a) truth (John 1:14)
8. Barnabas (Acts 4:36, 11:19–23)
9. abundance (Romans 5:17)
10. c) the law (Romans 6:14–15)
11. circumcision (Acts 15:3–11)
12. works (Romans 11:5–6, Ephesians 2:9)
13. taste (1 Peter 2:3)
14. hospitality (1 Peter 4:9–10)
15. c) grow in (2 Peter 3:18)

WEIGHT LIFTING

Snatch

1. sustain (Psalm 55:22)
2. rest (Matthew 11:28)
3. tree (1 Peter 2:24)
4. sorrows (Isaiah 53:4)
5. transgressors (Isaiah 53:12)
6. fulfil (Galatians 6:2)
7. called (1 John 3:1)
8. rest (Hebrews 4:9)
9. infirmities (Matthew 8:17)

Clean and Jerk

1. Peter (Matthew 14:28–29)
2. a) Philip (Acts 8:26–39)
3. c) condemnation (Romans 8:1)
4. faithful and just (1 John 1:9)
5. daily (Psalm 68:19)
6. "all your care," or anxiety (1 Peter 5:7)
7. d) the truth (John 8:31–32)
8. b) heirs (Galatians 4:7)
9. "all his benefits" (Psalm 103:2)
10. a) light (2 Corinthians 4:17)
11. intercession (Romans 8:34)
12. angels (Hebrews 1:13–14)
13. b) blessed (Titus 2:13)

14. free indeed (John 8:36)
15. "then I am strong" (2 Corinthians 12:10)

SWIMMING

Semifinals

1. thirst (John 4:14a)
2. scripture (John 7:38)
3. salvation (Isaiah 12:3)
4. renewed (2 Corinthians 4:16)
5. love (1 John 3:14)
6. right (Psalm 51:10)
7. washing (Titus 3:5)
8. holiness (Ephesians 4:24)
9. everlasting (John 4:14b)

Finals

1. new creature, or new creation
   (2 Corinthians 5:17)
2. b) stony (Ezekiel 36:26)

3. water and the Spirit (John 3:5)
4. a) Nicodemus (John 3:1–3)
5. eternal (John 17:3)
6. a little child (Matthew 18:1–3)
7. b) Peter (John 6:68–69)
8. a) 250 times (Matthew 13:23)
9. Zacchaeus (Luke 19:1–10)
10. Damascus (Acts 9:1–19)
11. c) Philippi (Acts 16:11–34)
12. the way, the truth (John 14:6)
13. b) "we love the brethren" (1 John 3:14)
14. more abundantly, or to the full
    (John 10:10)
15. gain (Philippians 1:21)

EQUESTRIAN

Dressage
1. lean (Proverbs 3:5)
2. princes (Psalm 118:9)
3. ashamed (Psalm 25:2)

4. good (Psalm 37:3)
5. blessed (Psalm 84:12)
6. snare (Proverbs 29:25)
7. afraid (Psalm 56:3)
8. strength (Psalm 46:1)
9. all times (Psalm 62:8)

Three-Day Event

1. b) Job (Job 13:15)
2. bow (Psalm 44:6–7)
3. d) shield (Psalm 3:3)
4. cursed (Jeremiah 17:5)
5. Shadrach, Meshach, and Abednego (Daniel 3:19–28)
6. b) riches (Mark 10:24)
7. chief priests, scribes, and elders (Matthew 27:41–43)
8. Mount Zion (Psalm 125:1)
9. a) Hezekiah (2 Kings 18:1–5, 20:1–6)
10. walls (Deuteronomy 28:52)
11. c) blessed (Psalm 40:4)
12. Saul (2 Samuel 22:1–3)
13. c) Egypt (Hebrews 11:24–27)
14. fool (Proverbs 28:26)
15. perfect (Isaiah 26:3)

BIATHLON

Cross-Country Skiing

1. lamp (Psalm 119:105)
2. sin (Psalm 119:11)
3. richly (Colossians 3:16)
4. hope (Romans 15:4)
5. wise (2 Timothy 3:15)
6. wisdom (James 1:5)
7. righteous (James 5:16)
8. will (1 John 5:14)
9. Bless (Luke 6:28)

Rifle Shooting

1. Berea (Acts 17:10–11)
2. d) truth (John 17:17)
3. approved (2 Timothy 2:15)
4. c) a twoedged sword (Hebrews 4:12)
5. door posts (Deuteronomy 11:18–20)
6. a) milk (1 Corinthians 3:1–2, 1 Peter 1:25–2:2)
7. Ezra (Nehemiah 8:1–12)
8. c) Daniel (Daniel 6:10–12)
9. intercession (Romans 8:26–27)
10. b) "hallowed be thy name" (Matthew 6:9)
11. seek, knock (Luke 11:9)
12. my name (John 14:13–14; 15:16; 16:23–24, 26)

13. daily (Matthew 6:11)
14. a widow (Luke 18:1–8)
15. b) without ceasing (1 Thessalonians 5:17)

BOXING

Preliminary Match
1. subjection (1 Corinthians 9:26–27)
2. crucified (Galatians 5:24)
3. disciple (Luke 14:33)
4. deny (Matthew 16:24)
5. Spirit (Galatians 5:16)
6. walls (Proverbs 25:28)
7. reign (Romans 6:12)
8. all things (1 Corinthians 9:25)
9. righteously (Titus 2:12)

Championship Match
1. gluttons (Proverbs 23:20–21)
2. b) Daniel (Daniel 1:8–12)

3. c) fasting (Mark 9:25–29)
4. Nazarite (Numbers 6:2–3)
5. d) Noah (Genesis 9:20–21)
6. the tongue (James 3:8)
7. being "slow to anger," or patient (Proverbs 16:32)
8. b) a corner of his robe (1 Samuel 24:1–11)
9. a roaring lion (1 Peter 5:8)
10. deacons (1 Timothy 3:8–11)
11. a) wisdom (Galatians 5:22–23)
12. a) Peter (Mark 10:28–31)
13. Felix (Acts 24:24–25)
14. mortify (Colossians 3:5)
15. "cut it off" (Matthew 5:30)

TUG OF WAR

Preliminary Round

1. crucified (Romans 6:6)
2. war (1 Peter 2:11)
3. Lie (Colossians 3:9)

4. good (Romans 7:18)
5. law (Romans 7:25)
6. evil (Romans 7:21)
7. will (1 Peter 4:2)
8. live (Galatians 2:20)
9. choose (Deuteronomy 30:19)

Finals

1. old (Romans 6:6, Ephesians 4:22, Colossians 3:9)
2. James and John (Luke 9:51–54)
3. b) He rebuked them (Luke 9:55–56)
4. c) please God (Romans 8:8)
5. a) Paul (Acts 23:1–5)
6. "by the renewing of your mind" (Romans 12:1–2)
7. every thought (2 Corinthians 10:5)
8. deceitful (Jeremiah 17:9, Ephesians 4:22)
9. b) Ananias (Acts 5:1–6)
10. wretched (Romans 7:24)
11. b) eating (Galatians 2:11–12)
12. the world (1 John 2:15)
13. d) "the deeds of the body" (Romans 8:13)
14. sure (2 Peter 1:10)
15. "the armour of light" (Romans 13:12)

FENCING

Foil

1. power (Romans 1:16)
2. for ever (1 Peter 1:25)
3. inspiration (2 Timothy 3:16)
4. pass away (Luke 21:33)
5. perfect (Psalm 19:7)
6. eternal life (1 John 5:13)
7. truth (John 17:17)
8. will (2 Peter 1:21)
9. meditation (Psalm 119:97)

Épée

1. honey (Psalm 119:103)
2. a hammer (Jeremiah 23:29)
3. a) a liar (Proverbs 30:6)
4. d) John (Revelation 22:8, 18–19)
5. b) Esaias, or Isaiah (Luke 4:16–21)
6. broken (John 10:34–35)
7. David (Luke 20:41–44)
8. d) the proverbs (Luke 24:44)
9. bread alone (Luke 4:4)
10. law (Psalm 119:1–174)
11. a) Josiah (2 Kings 22:1–23:3)
12. c) Paul (2 Peter 3:15–16)
13. grass or flower (Isaiah 40:8)

14. jot and tittle (Matthew 5:18)
15. holy (Romans 7:12)

ARCHERY

Semifinal Round
1. instruments (Romans 6:13)
2. common (1 Corinthians 10:13)
3. resist (1 Peter 5:8–9)
4. God (James 1:13)
5. deliver (Matthew 6:9, 13)
6. suffered (Hebrews 2:18)
7. godly (2 Peter 2:9)
8. entice (Proverbs 1:10)
9. flee (James 4:7)

Finals
1. d) "It is written" (Matthew 4:3–10)
2. forty (Matthew 4:1–2)

3. angels (Matthew 4:11)
4. a) "the father of" (John 8:42–44)
5. flee (2 Timothy 2:22)
6. c) Joseph (Genesis 39:1–12)
7. far (Proverbs 5:1–8)
8. his own lust, or evil desire (James 1:14)
9. c) the Holy Spirit (Acts 8:9–24)
10. to be rich (1 Timothy 6:9)
11. c) Elisha (2 Kings 5:1–27)
12. false prophets (Matthew 7:15)
13. d) his wife's (Job 2:9–10)
14. the armour of God (Ephesians 6:13)
15. watch and pray (Matthew 26:41, Mark 14:38)

SKIING

Slalom

1. plough, or plow (Luke 9:62)
2. love (Revelation 2:4)
3. haughty (Proverbs 16:18)
4. hear (Isaiah 59:2)

5. Return (Malachi 3:7)
6. strengthen (Luke 22:31–32)
7. attained (Philippians 3:16)
8. yoke (Galatians 5:1)
9. salvation (Hebrews 2:3)

Nordic Combined

1. the golden calf (Exodus 31:18–32:4)
2. b) foreign wives (1 Kings 11:1–4)
3. Hosea (Hosea 3:1–2)
4. b) Gomer (Hosea 1:2–3)
5. Uriah the Hittite (2 Samuel 11:2–5, 14–17)
6. "the joy of thy salvation" (Psalm 51:12)
7. a) Demas (2 Timothy 4:10)
8. d) Zoar (Genesis 19:1–22)
9. on rock (Luke 8:13)
10. a) young widows (1 Timothy 5:11–15)
11. bitterly (Matthew 26:75, Luke 22:61–62)
12. "Feed my sheep" (John 21:15–19)
13. John Mark (Acts 15:36–40)
14. profitable, or helpful (2 Timothy 4:11)
15. b) repent (Revelation 2:1–5)

WRESTLING

Semifinal Match
1. blood (Hebrews 12:4)
2. labour (Colossians 1:29)
3. peace (Romans 8:6)
4. stumblingblock (Romans 14:13)
5. devil (Ephesians 4:26–27)
6. sins (1 Timothy 5:22)
7. separate (Romans 8:35)
8. weapons (2 Corinthians 10:4)
9. strong (Ephesians 6:10)

Finals
1. b) Jacob (Genesis 32:22–30)
2. d) sin (Romans 7:15–17)
3. death (James 1:15)
4. friendship with the world (James 4:4)
5. c) corrupt (1 Corinthians 15:33)
6. his devices, or schemes (2 Corinthians 2:11)
7. "an angel of light" (2 Corinthians 11:14)
8. a) strange (1 Peter 4:12)
9. joy (James 1:2)
10. d) Elijah (1 Kings 19:1–4)
11. b) Thomas (John 11:14–16, 20:24–25)
12. fire (1 Corinthians 3:11–13)
13. peaceable (Hebrews 12:11)

14. his steps (1 Peter 2:21)
15. submit (James 4:7)

HURDLES

Preliminary Heat
1. evil (Romans 12:21)
2. word of God (1 John 2:14)
3. greater (1 John 4:4)
4. faith (1 John 5:4)
5. pillar (Revelation 3:12)
6. life (Revelation 2:7)
7. inherit (Revelation 21:7)
8. Son of God (1 John 5:5)
9. throne (Revelation 3:21)

Finals
1. a) all things (Philippians 4:13)
2. exceeding abundantly, or immeasurably more (Ephesians 3:20)
3. success (Joshua 1:8)

4. b) Gideon (Judges 7:1–25)
5. c) Daniel (Daniel 6:1–5, 28)
6. blessed (Job 42:12)
7. b) 30 years old (Genesis 41:14–46)
8. "but God meant it unto good" (Genesis 50:20)
9. serpents (or snakes) and scorpions
   (Luke 10:17–19)
10. a) "your names are written in heaven"
    (Luke 10:20)
11. cheek (Luke 6:29)
12. "evil for evil," or "wrong for wrong"
    (1 Thessalonians 5:15)
13. d) merciful (Luke 6:35–36)
14. our Lord Jesus Christ (1 Corinthians
    15:55–57)
15. conquerors (Romans 8:37)

BALANCE BEAM

Qualifying Routine
1. scriptures (1 Corinthians 15:3)

2. nations (Mark 13:10)
3. all (1 Timothy 2:1)
4. reconciled (Matthew 5:23–24)
5. hypocrite (Matthew 7:4–5)
6. cost (Luke 14:28)
7. servant (Mark 9:35)
8. firstborn (Colossians 1:18)
9. dead in Christ (1 Thessalonians 4:16)

Championship Routine

1. "Love the Lord thy God" (Matthew 22:37–38)
2. "Honour thy father and mother" (Ephesians 6:2)
3. d) holiness (Hebrews 12:14)
4. a) wisdom (Proverbs 4:7)
5. Elijah (1 Kings 17:8–16)
6. "upon the first day of the week"
   (1 Corinthians 16:1–2)
7. a) Macedonia (2 Corinthians 8:1–5)
8. a) her children and other relatives
   (1 Timothy 5:4)
9. sorrowful, or sad (Matthew 19:16–22)
10. repent (Acts 26:19–21)
11. d) "thank my God" (Romans 1:8)
12. Antioch (Acts 11:26)
13. c) Andrew (John 1:35–41)
14. Moses (Hebrews 11:24–25)
15. charity, or love (1 Corinthians 12:31, 13:1–8)

HIGH JUMP

First Jump
1. glory (1 Corinthians 10:31)
2. author (Hebrews 12:2)
3. thanks (Colossians 3:17)
4. good (1 Thessalonians 5:15)
5. heartily (Colossians 3:23)
6. man of God (1 Timothy 6:11)
7. holy (1 Peter 1:16)
8. love (Ephesians 5:1–2)
9. abound (Philippians 1:9–10)

Final Jump
1. a) wisdom (Proverbs 8:1–6)
2. "think on these things" (Philippians 4:8)
3. things above (Colossians 3:2)
4. c) peace (Psalm 34:14)
5. light (Ephesians 5:8)
6. narrow (Matthew 7:13–14)
7. c) living (Romans 12:1)
8. press (Philippians 3:14)
9. d) Peter (Acts 5:29)
10. d) Apollos (Acts 18:24–26)
11. Caleb and Joshua (Numbers 13:26–33, 32:12)
12. c) defile himself (Daniel 1:8)

13. childish things, or ways (1 Corinthians 13:11)
14. dung, or rubbish (Philippians 3:8)
15. heart, soul, mind, strength (Mark 12:30)

MARATHON

Warm-Up
1. patience (Hebrews 12:1)
2. faith (2 Timothy 4:7)
3. weary (Galatians 6:9)
4. continue (John 15:9)
5. tribulation (Acts 14:22)
6. disciples (John 8:31)
7. vine (John 15:4)
8. sons (Hebrews 12:7)
9. saved (Matthew 24:13)

Marathon
1. the cross (Hebrews 12:2)
2. Ephesus (Revelation 2:1–2)

3. b) "as a good soldier" (2 Timothy 2:3)
4. c) wild animals (2 Corinthians 11:23–28)
5. c) 3,000 (Acts 2:41–42)
6. seven (Acts 6:1–4)
7. the faith (1 Corinthians 16:13)
8. Egypt (Genesis 41:41)
9. a) in a dungeon (Genesis 41:14)
10. Joshua (Joshua 1:1–2, 7)
11. d) the wall of Jerusalem (Nehemiah 1:1–3, 6:15)
12. c) a sword (Nehemiah 4:18)
13. Job (James 5:11)
14. "the trying of your faith" (James 1:3)
15. "the Lord, and in the power of his might" (Ephesians 6:10)

CLOSING CEREMONY

Podium

1. appearing (2 Timothy 4:8)
2. life (James 1:12)
3. stars (Daniel 12:3)

4. reign (2 Timothy 2:12)
5. Lord (2 Corinthians 5:8)
6. glory (Romans 8:18)
7. great (Luke 6:35)
8. righteous (Matthew 13:43)
9. building (2 Corinthians 5:1)

National Anthem

1. Well done (Matthew 25:21, 23)
2. c) pleasures (Psalm 16:11)
3. good and perfect (James 1:17)
4. a) "the power of darkness" (Colossians 1:13)
5. a) Moses (Hebrews 11:24–26)
6. in paradise (Luke 23:39–43)
7. heaven (Matthew 5:11–12)
8. b) "a cup of cold water" (Matthew 10:42)
9. "the tree of life" (Revelation 21:27, 22:14)
10. sow and reap (Galatians 6:8)
11. d) this world (John 18:36)
12. moth and rust (Matthew 6:20)
13. b) serve (John 12:26)
14. adoption (Galatians 4:5–6)
15. his Son (1 John 5:11)

A NOTE ON SOURCES

There are a number of very good resources regarding the Olympic games, but the author found the following three most helpful in preparing this book:

The Complete Book of the Summer Olympics, by David Wallechinsky. Published by The Overlook Press, New York, 2000.

The Olympic Fact Book: A Spectator's Guide to the Winter Games, edited by George Cantor and Anne Janette Johnson. Published by Visible Ink Press, Detroit, 1997.

The International Olympic Committee Web Site, www.olympic.org.

LIKE BIBLE TRIVIA?

Then check out these great books from Barbour Publishing!

The Bible Detective by Carol Smith
Solve mysteries posed by a mixed-up story using biblical characters, places, and quotations.
ISBN 1-57748-838-5/Paperback/224 pages/$2.97

My Final Answer by Paul Kent
Thirty separate quizzes feature twelve multiple-choice questions each—and the questions get progressively harder!
ISBN 1-58660-030-3/Paperback/256 pages/$2.97

Bible IQ by Rayburn Ray
One hundred sections of ten questions each—and a systematic scoring system to tell you just how well you did.
ISBN 1-57748-837-7/Paperback/256 pages/$2.97

Test Your Bible Knowledge by Carl Shoup
Over 1,400 multiple-choice questions to test your mettle, tickle your funny bone, and tantalize your intellect.
ISBN 1-55748-541-0/Paperback/224 pages/$2.97

Fun Facts About the Bible by Robyn Martins
Challenging and intriguing Bible trivia—expect some of the answers to surprise you!
ISBN 1-55748-897-5/Paperback/256 pages/$2.97

Available wherever books are sold.
Or order from:

Barbour Publishing, Inc.
P.O. Box 719
Uhrichsville, OH 44683
www.barbourbooks.com

If you order by mail add $2.00 to your order for shipping.
Prices subject to change without notice.